JERRY'S
BOOK OF
WISDOM

To: My dear friend

I'm proud of you + The

love you much

Apostle Larry D Anderson

JERRY'S BOOK OF WISDOM

FOR THOSE WHO HAD NO FATHER AT HOME

by JERRY D. ANDERSON

Trilogy Christian Publishers

A Wholly Owned Subsidiary of Trinity Broadcasting Network

2442 Michelle Drive

Tustin, CA 92780

10 9 8 7 6 5 4 3 2 1

Library of Congress Cataloging-in-Publication Data is available.

ISBN 979-8-88738-029-2

ISBN 979-8-88738-030-8 (ebook)

MR. ANDERSON'S PROVERBIAL WISDOM FOR MEN, WOMEN, AND TEENS

1. Honor and respect God.

2. Love your wife, and don't forget why you married her.

3. Treat everyone special because they are, and so are you.

4. When you smile, the world will smile back at you.

5. Include every nationality in your life; if you don't, you limit your experience.

6. Respect those in authority. Never gossip about those over you; it will get back to them, never as you have stated. Your jealous co-worker will make sure of that.

7. Read more. You need to stay aware of current events. Reading will increase your net worth, and it will make your conversations interesting. Read a little about everything. Study the Bible; it will keep you balanced. Read books on how to be a better friend, how to add preventive maintenance to items you own, and how to be a better all-around spouse.

8. Don't live to eat but eat to live. Eat foods that will not clog up your veins as you get older. You will be faced with this dilemma.

9. Never hit your spouse. Keep your hands to yourself. When you become that angry, shut up and walk away. Take a drive and listen to some easy music or music that makes you happy.

10. Kiss your spouse before you leave each morning. Tell them you love them each day. Greet your spouse when they come home from work. Serve them every chance you get. Never make them the object of the joke at the family gathering. Compliment them when the family is around. Respect their friends and their family. Treat your spouse like royalty; you will reap what you sow. Tell them you are sorry when you mess up. You will mess up quite often; get used to it because you are a human being, and you are not perfect. Love and respect yourself. Don't put up with people just because you want their friendship. When you know they are not good for you, look for better friends. When

you have someone in your life that wants to be your friend, give them a chance. When you get older, you will be glad you did. Be a good friend and tell your friend when they are great and when they are not. Let them know when they offend you; tell them that they hurt you. If you don't, they will lose respect, and you will harbor unforgiveness and resentment that will cause you to eventually kick them to the curb. Long-term relationships need correction periodically, so make sure you agree to correct one another instead of throwing away the years of investment that you both have placed into the relationship.

11. So-called geeks are smart people. You will be so glad that you were nice to them when you are older. They may one day interview you for a job or even be your boss. Be kind to everyone, especially your neighbor, because one day you will need them.

12. When communicating, make sure you are a great, active listener, and you are empathetic. This will make people feel special and valuable around you. Ever talking only about you and yours make people sick of you quickly.

13. When eating at the table, try not to bring bad news. It's a time of celebration where joy and good news is to be the priority. By the way, if someone is always bringing you tons of bad news, tell them you are not a garbage can and to stop it because it makes you miserable. You need to hear good things from them to enjoy their presence.

14. Put your hand over your mouth when you cough, sneeze, are chewing, and when you burgh. It's respectful and considerate of others.

15. When you have a call on your phone, please talk quietly if you have to answer. No one wants to hear your conversation. That's inconsiderate. Turn your phone off when you are in the movie theater. People did not pay for a ticket to hear you talk on your phone.

16. Take walks in the park and enjoy the fresh air, the trees, looking at the ducks, and the children laughing and playing. It really is wonderful and therapeutic.

17. Never drive with your knees, and please don't text while driving. Never put makeup on, drink, use drugs, or use your phone while driving. You could seriously lose your life or hurt someone else. This happens more often than you could imagine.

18. Watch your drink when you go to parties. Nowadays, people place things in your drink just for a kick. Never try any (smoking) drug anywhere. Once you have taken one puff, you can be addicted for life. The so-called ride-or-die or ignorant friend/dealer knows this; that's why he will offer it for free the first time. Afterward, it could cost you your paychecks, your job, business, inheritance, all self-respect, complete savings, your family, and finally, your life.

19. Ladies, if you know nothing about a car, make sure you learn to check your oil and transmission fluid, check your tires before you leave each morning, and have someone to make sure antifreeze is in your radiator. This will save you lots of money and headaches in the long run. There are companies that have professional mechanics who will inspect a car before you purchase it for about 200 dollars. Get it checked out before you buy it.

20. Married men, be careful with your compliments. Some simply will not take them right. They will think you want them. However, most will know how to properly receive them; this wisdom will also go for married women as well.

21. Young ladies, don't sit in a man's lap. You will send the wrong signal to many young men.

22. Young ladies, never go to a man's house if you don't know him well. In fact, it's very wise to meet people at a restaurant for lunch before you trust them to come into your home for anything. If you live with a man and you are not married, this

will highly eliminate his chances of marrying you. In hindsight, you will regret this tremendously. Men, if you cohabitate with someone's daughter without marrying her, you are completely disrespecting her family. If she is good enough to shack with, she's good enough to marry.

23. When dining with him or her, if you drink anything or smoke dope, it could cause you to drop many of your principles, boundaries, and inhibits. Be careful. The offer could be a trick. Many unwanted pregnancies happen because of this.

24. Take a needy person to get them food rather than give them money if you can.

25. Be kind to the poor; remember it could have been you.

26. Respect your parents. Never cuss your parents out. They may not have been the best, but they are your parents. Forgive and respect them. This will always make your life happier.

27. Report abuse to the authorities. We have trained personnel for those folks. Never put up with people abusing you. Children, make sure it is legitimate abuse. For example: Are they hitting you with their fist, burning you with cigarettes, improperly touching you, having any sex with you, chaining you up, locking you in closets, or cussing you out every single day? That's abuse; go to someone that will listen to you and call the police.

28. Women, if a man is slapping you, keeping you from having friends, making you perform sex acts against your will, taking your money, threatening to kill you, being always unkind to you, that's abuse! No matter how much they say they love you, it's not the truth. Get away from them ASAP. Get professional help. Police authorities and YWCA can help you.

29. If someone in authority tries to coerce you into doing something that is against the law, let them know you will report them if they don't stop. Take care of business.

30. A women's long hair is her glory. Men love long hair also.

31. Never park beside a large vehicle at night. Gas up and get your shopping done, at reputable places in the daylight, if possible. There are some neighborhoods you do not want to be shopping at all, especially at night. It's simply too dangerous; you could get robbed or carjacked.

32. If you have a car that you don't want scratched or dented up, park your vehicle a little ways from other cars.

33. Marry a person that loves you as much as you love them. If they are selfish, you will suffer emotionally when the honeymoon wears off. Marry your best friend, someone who will give you their last, if you need it. Don't marry a person for good looks and a great shape only. This will all change after the years go by. Their character, love, and compatibility will sustain your marriage because the physique will change. You get my point. Men, don't prepare to dump your spouse because she has had children, and the shape isn't there anymore. Remember, you had a major part in that change. In fact, for both of you, look at their parents, and you can pretty much see how your spouse will look in their later years. Also, before you get married, have your fiancé promise you they will work on excellent character traits for the rest of their life. Also, whatever you did to get them to marry you, that is exactly what you will need to continue when you are married and so much more.

34. Don't buy a new car if you don't have to; even if you purchase a vehicle that's one year old, it will smell new, but it will cost approximately 10,000.00 dollars cheaper. When you drive a new car off the lot, the value diminishes by thousands of dollars instantly. By the way, take a man with you that knows plenty about cars. So many women have been taken advantage of.

35. When purchasing a home, always go for the lowest *fixed interest* rate. Make sure the neighborhood is not too close to a gas station or apartments. Drive through the neighborhood to see what it's like at night. There may be close neighbors that stay out all night, making all kinds of noises.

36. Everyone's personality needs improving but always be yourself. There's not one person that can be a better you. Don't live your life as a copycat. Be happy being nobody but the better and best you.

37. Invest in a hobby. You will thank me for that tip.

38. Go to college, if at all possible, if you don't learn at least two trades. These days, you will need it. By the way, my research reveals that America is worth about 200 trillion or more. What part of this will you establish a needed business to get? I call this the Promised Land. Many should start their own business and set it into motion once adequate clientele and administration are established. Do your due diligence, and don't leave your full-time job prematurely.

39. Always give people a good strong handshake. Not some jelly something. Look people in the eyes when you are talking to them. Hold your head up and live your life with dignity.

40. Never give a person the opportunity to tell you "no" when they don't have the authority, no way.

41. When you fail, learn from it; that's part of life and part of any endeavor. You will fail. Get up, learn from it and start over. Every day God offers us a fresh new opportunity to get it right, start over and move forward. Nothing is so devastating to where it warrants hurting or harming yourself physically. Nothing.

42. Love enhances everything in your life.

43. Knowledge will never determine your level of maturity; love will.

44. To serve in your home requires us to do what is needed and not necessarily what we only want to do.

45. A genuine person is one that walks in love.

46. God will never give up on you, so don't be so quick to give up on others.

47. Life is not always fair; it's tough. Therefore you will have times of sorrow, loss, disappointment, and bewilderment. But none of these times will last forever. They come to past. Morn for a time but not forever; if you do, you will find yourself stuck in it, and you will need someone to come and get you out of that rut. Be careful.

48. Every morning, you can choose to be happy, joyful, angry, sad, miserable, or boring. You chose to be the best and enjoy your day. Don't let anyone steal your joy!

49. Quit trying to make people feel sorry for you.

50. Be known for being positive, forgiving, loving, encouraging, and one who gladly serves and honors all people. Don't be racist and a respecter of persons. That's plain horrible.

51. Rejoice when people rejoice, weep when they weep. Many times you don't have to say anything; just being there when people need support means everything.

52. Don't try to support too many friends. You don't have the time, especially when you are married. Friendship costs a lot of time to invest in and nurture. One best friend or two good close friends will be great for you.

53. Check on your friends periodically. You must nurture the relationship, or you will lose it.

54. Cosign for no one. This will protect a good relationship. Some people may want to come live with you for a while. It may be better for you to just loan them money to stay in a hotel. Staying with you could be the worst thing that could have happened. Don't let everyone use your car, your mower, or your tools. Most folks don't treat your personal things like you do.

55. Let no relative come to live with you without the consent of your spouse, even if it's your momma. Also, if you agree, make sure a time limit is given and signed. Make sure rules are set, agreed upon, and signed.

56. When you lend money, it may be good to know to whom, or you may not get it all back or none at all.

57. When at the gas pump today, you could easily mistake diesel for unleaded. The hoses are on the same pump housing. Be careful.

58. Don't drive on ice at all. If you do, deflate your tires just a little and drive very slowly.

59. Be kind to your animals. They do everything possible to make you happy, and they do a great job at it.

60. When you have a bad cold or the flu, stay at home. Don't get out until your doctor release you. Don't just spread the virus to others knowingly. (Wear a mask if you have to go out, and cough under your arm.)

61. With a house with high vaulted ceilings, you can save on utilities in the winter by using space or tower heaters. Set your thermostat at 72 degrees and carry the heater to the family room, then to the bedrooms. It will save hundreds for those that use only gas. Always be very careful where you place the heaters. You may not want to place one in a child's room at all.

62. Place fire and smoke detectors in your home and at least one carbon monoxide detector.

63. Buy plastic plug-ins at your local hardware store and place them into the unused electrical sockets in your home to keep children safe.

64. Tell your teen never to cook anything on the stove when they come home late. Tell them to use the microwave, eat cereals or make a cold-cut sandwich.

65. Always, when cooking, turn the handle of the skillet or pot toward the stove. This safety measure will save your children from danger.

66. Never discipline your child when you are in public; you might get away with a pinch. When you are angry, you will mess up. Wait until you cool off because they will take you there.

67. Hello, my son/daughter, please forgive me for not being there for you and for not being the ideal father that I could have been. Forgive me for the things I have done that hurt you. Please forgive your daddy. Forgive me for hurting your mother. Please forgive me for not being there to play with you, protect you, be at your graduations, and at special moments at school. I did not know how important these things were to you. I am so very sorry.

68. Trust people; everyone is not irresponsible; all men are not bad people. You place yourself in a self-made prison when you stop trusting. Allow people to prove to you if they are unreliable. To enjoy the fullness of life, you will have to extend your heart to trust people, even though they will disappoint you. Remember, no one's perfect, not even you.

69. When it's cold, put on clothes that will keep you warm. This is not a time to be cool, ultra-fashionable, and irresponsible.

70. Eat breakfast, lunch, and dinner. Take care of yourself.

71. Don't fill yourself with too much caffeine; it will deceive your mind into thinking you need no rest. Get the proper amount of sleep each day so your life (spirit, soul, and body) can be fully rested, restored, and healthy. You will need to be your optimum to be creative and sharp. Please love yourself that much.

72. To be a great friend, get information that will teach you both how to be friends. This means getting a book that will equip you and your friend. You both need to agree to read it and apply the wisdom to your friendship investment.

73. Brush and floss twice a day, so your teeth and gums will be healthy. Don't be too harsh on your gums. Too much candy and gum will destroy your teeth.

74. If you place chemicals in your hair, you will need wigs and weaves real soon. This will cost lots of money. Treat your hair with extreme care. Ladies, manicured nails are your trademark, it makes you look great.

75. Everyday life comes automatically with a level of stress that you can handle. But watch for what you allow that takes you overboard. Exercise and great hobbies relieve stress. Overload of stress can come in the form of people or career choices. Be careful what jobs you choose and the friends you make.

76. Treat everyone the way you want to be treated.

77. Start a savings, checking, or retirement account as soon as possible. Don't touch it either.

78. Continue to do what is right, even if you have to be alone temporarily.

79. Being part of a gang and selling drugs could easily place your spouse, children, mother, father, and brother's life in jeopardy. When you don't do what is demanded of you, you will pay, or your completely innocent loved ones are subject to pay.

80. When you are practicing wrong actions, it's like sowing seeds in your life. You are setting a law into play. If you sow good seeds, you will reap good things, but if you sow bad things, you will reap bad and harmful situations in your life. You are setting your guaranteed course for your future. This practice will also set your children up to receive what you have started. This is why so many bad things happen in the next generation's life.

81. Wash your hands often during the day. This will get rid of many germs that you come into contact with. We pick them up all day on every door knob. These germs can make you sick.

82. Just because a person is educated by our system does not mean they are ethical and have morals. Some are foolish, unwise, and will turn you away from God.

83. When you need general services, go with a reputable company. Check reviews on your computer. Get yourself a computer and be on the cutting edge with this. There are awesome and necessary benefits in research.

84. When you are old enough to vote, vote for the person or party that honors God and the Bible the most. This can be a difficult decision because many politicians put up a godly and moral front so they can get your vote. Pray, and God will lead you. Check out those that will honor godly principles the most.

85. As a young adult trying to start on your own, buy a good used car for cash if you can; don't try to handle a car note because the rent and other bills may get just a little too much.

86. Keep your vehicle and home clean; you will always appreciate what you buy if you keep it clean. You don't have to purchase another vehicle each time you pay your current one off. A paid-off car can be a sign of some established wealth. You have no idea what it feels like to have a paid-off mortgage. (Make an intentional aim for this.)

87. Don't always look for the cheapest items to buy. It will be more feasible to pay a little more for some things because this will keep you from having to purchase the same thing again too soon.

88. Garage sales will help you save lots of money on items and children's clothes. Kids grow out of them so quickly, so don't buy too many of them retail. Go early to the sales so you can get better bargains. You don't have to spend thousands of dollars to get certain jewelry, etc.; you can get items that look very similar to the name brands very cheap. Rich people do this also.

89. Wash, starch, and iron your own clothes. This will ensure a neat appearance and save you lots of money.

90. Young folk, start working as soon as possible. If you do, this will begin to help you get ready for life on your own. You need to learn how to work hard. This will be the only way to get the

better things you want out of life. Lazy people will always go for the shortcut or fall for all the get-rich schemes (gambling, stealing, robbing, etc.). Make a legitimate life for yourself.

91. Gambling may seem enjoyable and entertaining, but it is extremely dangerous. The most addictive moments are when you win. It makes you spend a hundred times as much to get that thrill again. It is best to get your entertainment elsewhere. People have become addicted and lost everything, and many have harmed themselves because they lost their marriages, homes, and businesses.

92. When you are in the public eye, set examples that will keep people safe, especially the children. Watch what you say because you may wish you hadn't when you are older. You don't have to be opinionated. You don't have to say something about everything. Also, don't be one to always fight other people's fights. Mind your own business.

93. Never use profanity. It's the devil's language, and it makes you a potty mouth.

94. Sorcery and witchcraft are dangerous. Beware! If you are trapped in its clutches, see a church ministry that can minister deliverance to you. This can be a phenomenal help for you and your children. Deliverance ministries are found more so in non-denominational churches. If you are hearing voices, seeing ghosts, or hearing things drop in your home, see a church that specializes in deliverance ministry. They will help you deal with these issues.

95. When you have been close to people with a bad cold, go home and spray saline in your nostrils, according to the directions, and goggle with salt and water. For those with high blood pressure, be careful with the salt solution. (See your physician for this advice.)

96. Those with high blood pressure can eat better, exercise, and be able to many times get off their medicines. Make sure you

are directed by your doctor. But if you just won't eat like you should, please *take your medicine*. Good salads and exercise will help decrease your numbers.

97. Listen to your body; many times, it will tell you when you need to adjust yourself. When you eat something, and you become dizzy, or your stomach becomes upset, this is your body talking, don't ignore it. Make changes.

98. Listen to your conscious; most of the time, it will cause discomfort in your heart when you are experiencing something not safe for you.

99. Celebrate every holiday. If you work hard, you need to play hard. Keep a budget but celebrate each holiday with zeal, gratitude, and appreciation. If no one on your street is celebrating, you do. Don't allow current circumstances and situations to steal the enjoyment that holidays bring.

100. Immorality will destroy you. The Bible will teach you morality. In this world's system, everyone is right in their own eyes. But the Bible will keep a standard before you that will keep you safe, ethical, balanced, and moral.

101. Being a part of some team in school is an all-around good for your development.

102. Take lots of pictures and make many videos when you are younger. These will be invaluable as you get older. Make sure you keep names and phone numbers.

103. Life is not all about you. You are here to help others become successful. You are here to serve and to make this world a better place. Make sure you take time to sacrifice and serve others. This keeps you from being lonely and selfish.

104. Change is inevitable if you want to be successful. This goes for marriage, work, business, etc. For a person to say, "I won't change for anyone," is to lack understanding.

105. If you know what you are practicing is wrong, don't try to make people accept your error. Never be found trying to make right behavior wrong and wrong behavior right. That's even worse. Follow the Lord, and He will help you do what's right if you humble yourself and ask Him too. Then, stick to what is right until you are loosed from your captivity and deception. Freedom will come.

106. Don't agree with the adage "try everything once" or "do whatever feels good." This can lead to great devastation in your life. Let me slip this in: Keep the cookie in your cookie jar until he puts a ringy on your fingy. If you make him wait, he will be glad to do what is right.

107. Yes, there is a spiritual side to life. Only God can properly guide you with this. Any other source of spiritual guidance will lead you into spiritual error. Trained pastors will be your best source of wisdom in this area.

108. Smell the food that you buy before you cook or eat it, especially meats. It could be outdated and spoiled. Many times you can catch it if you take a moment to smell it.

109. Tell your doctor if you have allergies. If you think that you have grown out of them, tell your doctor anyway. There is great caution that must be taken. Take meds according to instructions. Do what your doctor says. If you don't, why waste your time and theirs.

110. You are very valuable; everything seen and unseen can be replaced but you; therefore, you deserve the good, better, and best that life has to offer you.

111. Learn to cook boiled foods such as beans, cabbage, greens, and peas. Baked chicken, turkey, and fish will be good for you. Eating greasy foods all the time is not good for you.

112. If you have a home or a car, get a set of extra keys. This will save you a great headache if you do.

113. Write all of your pin numbers, user numbers, and passwords down and place them in a safe place. Don't try to remember them all. You will forget some.

114. Learn how to swim early in life, but get a professional to help you.

115. Learn to use a GPS system. Maps are good but, in some cases, are outdated.

116. Be positive, at least most of the time. People hate being around a constant complainer. Some people think that constantly sharing bad news is what you want to hear. This is far from the truth. Actually, misery loves company.

117. Young men, always be kind to ladies. You never have a right to hit a woman. Never!

118. Take well-calculated risks. You will need it to get to higher grounds in life. Fear will keep you in mediocrity.

119. When you stand in front of an audience, know that everyone gets nervous; just focus on what you have to say, and the fear will begin to subside. If you drop something or if you begin to shake, don't worry about it. Pick up what you dropped and continue as if nothing happened. As it relates to the shaking, 99 percent of the people will not detect it. The other one percent knows that those symptoms come with having the guts to tackle an audience.

120. You don't have to have something to say about everything. This is called being opinionated. Be quiet sometimes.

121. When you are riding with others, listen to them and/or listen to music. You don't have to talk all the time when you are with people. Actually, a person who talks too much and exaggerates reveals how much they don't know and lie a lot. Enjoy the sound of peace and just enjoy being safe in one another's presence. People that love you, even if you both are silent, love you the most. They feel safe with you.

122. When you listen to what people are saying, you will find out what they like and enjoy. This will give you clues as to what gifts to buy them. By the way, if you don't know what gift to buy, gift cards are a great time-saver.

123. If you want to save gasoline, buy a four or six-cylinder car or truck instead of an eight-cylinder care truck.

124. Lock your car when you are going inside to purchase gas. Also, don't leave infants in the car. By the way, if anyone riding with you is jeopardizing safety, stop and put them out if they won't stop. That is your mature responsibility.

125. When you are not using a light in your home, cut it off. This saves money.

126. Don't cheat on your taxes, and make sure you file each year. This will come back to haunt you.

127. Eating and looking at horror movies before bed will cause nightmares and loss of needed sleep. This will instill fear in people as well.

128. When using a knife, always cut downward on a table or any flat surface. If you use a knife to cut something in your hand and you are cutting upwards, you could easily hurt yourself.

129. When using a drill or electrical saw, make sure you are trained well. These items can be very dangerous if you have no training.

130. When playing baseball, watch the person that is at bat very closely. If they sling the bat after they hit the ball, you need to be ready to get out of the way.

131. Drink plenty of water or Gatorade when you are playing or working outside. By the way, drinking at least four glasses of water daily has been proven to prevent prostate cancer by 50 percent.

132. Put a visor or cap on your head when you are under extreme sunlight and in very hot conditions.

133. Always look for (genuine) things to laugh about. Look at comedy very often; it's good for you. It's said that fifteen minutes of gut-wrenching laughter can guarantee the same relief and satisfaction as eight hours of deep sleep.

134. Wear shoes that fit you well. Don't buy shoes that are too loose or too tight.

135. Children, don't play in or around any type of trunk or closet that locks when they are closed.

136. Eat vegetables and fruits; they are good and healthy for you.

137. People are drawn to excellence. You will never be ignored or denied when you are excellent.

138. You will need to constantly forgive if you are to help society become a better place.

139. When people are wrong, don't ever agree or condone their error. Pray for them.

140. Beware on TV; just because an applause or laughter machine is played behind a statement, it does not make it genuinely funny. In fact, if you hear an applause or laughter machine, pay attention; there may be some deception in what you are seeing and hearing. By the way, watching too many commercials will stop you from enjoying what you already have.

141. If you are running a cash register, don't let anyone confront you about giving them change when the drawer is open. This is an age-old trick to confuse you and trick you into giving them more change them you should. They will go on and on, telling you how pretty you are; watch it; they may be trying to deceive you.

142. Young men, don't take a girl's money and gifts just because she's desperate and wants a man. This will be fine if you have a girlfriend and you both are giving one another's gifts. Some gifts also carry invisible strings attached to them. Watch it. Be

very careful and concerned when someone all of a sudden buys you an expensive gift for no reason at all. Give it back.

143. Learn to play all the different kinds of sports. It will be a blessing for you when you are older. You will be fun to be around, and your children will love it.

144. Let others have their way sometimes. You don't have to have your way all of the time.

145. Smile, and the world will smile back at you. People will also want to be around you. Frowning and looking mean will run people away from you. Smiling makes people feel safe, accepted, wanted, respected, and honored.

146. Be friendly, and people will be friendly to you.

147. Write down when great things happen in your life. You need to refer back to them to see how good God has been and how fruitful your life has been.

148. Always give people grace to make mistakes. No one is perfect. Don't be so hard and yourself and others. Learning is a process.

149. It does not take many different world philosophies to develop a happy and fulfilled life. It will, however, necessitate God's basic absolutes. They are called *truths*. The Bible holds *truth*.

150. If you are confused about what you should do, ask someone that is very wise, learned, and skilled in what you have questions about. Get off the pride. Also, remember, you don't refer to a talk show host about biblical wisdom; you talk to one that has been trained in that area. Football professionals are not to be your professional counselors for raising your children. My point, too many people listen to the wrong people for advice that has not been trained in the appropriate areas. Young people, your friends are only in their teens. They don't know as much as you think they know about life.

151. Young men, especially, make sure you open doors, inflate tires and pump gas for your mother and for the girls in your life. Male chivalry will never become outdated. Make sure you pull the chairs out at the table, let the lady sit down, and then have them scoot up to the table with the chair.

152. Young people, you are to say "yes ma'am" and "yes sir" to those who are your elders.

153. Be thankful and grateful for everything people give and do for you. No one has to do anything for you. Thank God for answering every prayer after you pray; this releases a powerful blessing of multiplication in your life, and God and people will want to do more for you.

154. Young people, you are to never call your mother, father, uncles, or aunts by their first name. You should call them Uncle John, Aunt Sue, etc. Call your parents Mom, Momma, Mother, Dad, Father, and Daddy. Other adults are to be called Mr. or Mrs.

155. Never make jokes, inwardly hate, or laugh at the less fortunate, depraved, poor, or handicapped.

156. To be successful in the culture you live in and to be able to be respected, *you must dress to impress.* If you dress like a thug or a gang member, you will be treated that way by mainstream America. If you talk like a thug or if you come off as the cool slang champion, you can forget about getting great jobs that pay excellent wages. You are a very valuable human being. If you present yourself as something less, why get upset with people that look for high self-esteem and excellence from you. Wearing pants that hang below your rear end tells every person of excellence that you hate who you are. That picture depicts a 150-pound, two-year-old wearing a dirty, soiled cloth diaper. This is epic confusion.

157. Honor those that leave home and place their lives in danger to serve the community.

158. Also, honor those that have given their lives for our freedom and for the advancement of science.

159. Respect the pastors that serve in your community. They have a very tough job trying to be under-shepherds for the people God has given them to serve. So goes the churches, so goes the family, so goes the family, so goes the nation.

160. Check on the elderly in your family and your community periodically.

161. Being late means someone has to wait.

162. Being early means you are showing the value and appreciation of your invite and for the relationship. Being on time is good, but being early is much better.

163. As it relates to being single, establish yourself to be complete, whole, and happy with yourself.

164. Get enough sleep. Eight hours is ideal. Not enough sleep is very dangerous for you. It is the major cause of depression.

165. Being affirmed and appreciated are two of the greatest human needs.

166. Build intimacy by revealing deep, positive, and meaningful things that touch your heart.

167. Sharing all your feelings with others deepens your relationships. Reciprocation will multiply warm and golden experiences.

168. To be known is to truly reveal yourself to others. How can someone know how to love you 100 percent if you don't tell them what makes you feel amazing.

169. Being hard on yourself means you can be difficult to be around sometimes. You are not to demand perfection from sinful humanity. We are not programmed robots. At the levels we are all at, we are doing our very best.

170. Most celebrations mean that you are honoring people. It reveals and deepens the love and appreciation for one another. It means you are willing to make sacrifices to enhance the emotional health of others.

171. Yesterday is history, tomorrow is a mystery, but today is a gift, and that's why it's called the present.

172. When you are around people, become a good questioner and a great listener.

173. Ideas can be diamonds in the rough.

174. Invite someone to a cup of coffee, tea, breakfast, or lunch. Cherish those who are most important in your life.

175. It's said that in a lifetime, it would be next to a miracle to acquire two close friends. Those who will stick it out through the years, sharing your sorrows and joys, taking good and bad, forgiving and being forgiven.

176. Greet friends with genuine enthusiasm. Greet them with a kind countenance, warm welcome, and express interest in their well-being. Friendliness is great and contagious.

177. Show that you can keep secrets and become trustworthy. You will be granted great levels of trust. The trust of a friend is a terrible thing to waste.

178. Keep short accounts. Good friends know that everyone has shortcomings and are willing to forgive in a split second whenever possible.

179. Believe in the best of people. When things inevitably go wrong, human beings tend to take the situation personally. They are too quick to draw extreme conclusions before they have a clear understanding of what actually transpired. Be unbiased until you know all the facts and before thinking the worst.

180. Look for what you can give in a relationship. Friendship is a two-way street, or at least it should be. Support should be

reciprocated. You will call on them, and they will need to call on you, sometimes. Don't forget to be a gracious receiver. This is what relationship and friendship are all about.

181. Be aware of the power of the human touch. Don't hug people that insist they are not huggers, but a small token of physical affection goes a long way. Studies show that there is undeniable healing in physical touches. You can use high–fives, a pat on the shoulder, or a warm, firm handshake. It's a signal of closeness and caring that results in friendship. A simple human touch can mean so much. It can also be a sign of acceptance.

182. Giving token gift. Consider maintaining a friendship budget; so you can give small well-timed gifts of affection or appreciation. Just being your token of appreciation.

183. Learn to compliment people. One person said, "I can live a whole week on one compliment." If you can't think of something nice to say, think harder; or you can find many on your computer or smartphone. We tend to provide them much more for children, but adults need them just as much.

184. Become an active listener. Shakespeare said, "Give every man thy ear but few thy voice." In such a busy world, one of the greatest gifts we could give someone is our undivided attention. Listen without thinking about what you are going to do next. Be empathetic and focus on their eyes and mannerisms, the factors that speak louder than words.

185. Be vulnerable. Be the encourager and allow yourself to be encouraged because life will take you through ups and downs. It takes courage to let your guards down and let your needs known. Let your friends know that you need their support.

186. Text and write notes to people. Text messaging and notes are short and sweet; everyone enjoys receiving them.

187. Ask for God's help. Friends are God's gift to us along this path. They love us, laugh with us, comfort us, and they encourage us. If you don't have a friend, your life can be very lonely. When

God gives us a good friend, He is hoping that we don't toss them aside at the first sign of discontent. We must realize they are a treasure from God. Ask God to give us a deep appreciation for friends that decorate our life. Ask Him to show us how to nurture the relationships. Read about characteristics and the elements of friendship. This makes our hearts and minds sensitive to great friendships.

188. Make yourself available to help your friend when he needs you. Most people are reluctant to ask for help because of the busyness that we all experience in this life. Be sensitive to schedules. People may not have the same level of together time. Some may simply have busier schedules. Some relationships may not be worth your pursuing because of the limited parameters. Their availability is just not there.

189. Be sensitive to preferences. As a young person, friendship means agreeing about everything, looking alike, etc., but adults may have to go to their favorite movie theatre sometimes, etc. Strive to be flexible whenever possible. Flexibility and accommodation bring growth and appreciation.

190. Be inquisitive. It's human nature to want to know. The best way to know someone is to ask questions. People are like wrapped packages filled with unique treasures.

191. Get into the habit of asking leading questions that cannot be answered with a regular yes. For example, "Yes, that must have been exciting; what were you feeling at the time?" Be grateful for a friend that is willing to be open and will share with you.

192. Look for common interest. Long-term compatibility in a friendship needs to have at least two areas of common interest to develop. The more important the common interests are to you, the more you will share. Share interests like music, art, spiritual beliefs, and certain hobbies. Same-age mothers bring about good cohesiveness to the relationship. Friends that play together stay together.

193. Be willing to introduce your friend to others; don't be concerned about them liking your new friend more than you or less than you. It is an honor to be introduced to a group of good friends that your friend can be part of. You will never know how the acquaintance can benefit them.

194. Use email during the day to share personal thoughts, funny moments, and ups and downs in your day, all of which strengthen intimacy.

195. Practice speaking positively. Most people think negatively, but you want to be an optimistic person. If you think more on the pessimistic side, read material that will help you be more positive. In friendship, negativity will bring others down.

196. Be careful not to criticize another friend. People will be wary *of your loyalty* to them if you are always talking about or criticizing your friend.

197. If you know you are suffering from feelings of fear, guilt, anger, failure, or even shame, as it relates to past experiences, get help. These feelings are likely to intensify and affect current relationships. The healthier you are emotionally, the healthier your friendships will be.

198. Be there when things get tough. Be a faithful friend when they are going through a hard time.

199. Love unconditionally. Unconditional love is an amazing concept that gives a sense of worth and freedom. This is a superhuman virtue. The characteristics are patience, kindness, humility, and keeping records of no wrong. It means accepting and loving people for who they are, plus faults as well as strengths. Unconditional love inspires limitless ways to grow.

200. Clip articles and save coupons. This will help your friend save money.

201. Show up and show support. If your friend is speaking, acting, or participating in an event, show up and support them. Even

if their child is in the event, show up and share your friend's feelings of pride and accomplishments. As a result, watch your friendship grow. Sacrifice some time and show you care by being there. This is what true friends do.

202. Commit to spiritual growth. When we have a vital and growing relationship with God, it is easier to have vital and growing relationships with others. The Bible gives us wisdom, comfort, and guidance for life's bumpy roads. The more we fill our minds and hearts with God's Word, the more *secure* we become as human beings. When you feed your soul, not only will you grow, but your friendships will as well.

203. Tell your friend you love spending time with them. Tell them, "I am a better person because of you." Everyone desires to be appreciated and affirmed. People don't always know these things unless you open your heart and tell them. It's one of the deepest human needs.

204. Work things out when it comes to disagreements and conflicts. Don't resort to silent treatments or the cold shoulder. Don't allow yourself to blow up and lose control by yelling and punching your friend. Many people hate confrontation. They will disappear and withdraw when things happen. Open up and be honest about what's bothering you.

205. It's always sad to lose friends, but many times people change, move out of town, or begin to enjoy different activities that serve very different interests.

206. Be open to experiences of all nationalities and different people. Don't settle to live in one limited box.

207. Choose friends that support the positive things in your life.

208. Too many people suffer from sleep deprivation. This will cause irritations, low creativity, forgetfulness, mistakes, withdrawal, depression, etc.

209. Beware of too much technology in your life. This can distance you from valuable relationships.

210. Chemistry, the interaction of one personality with another, rapport any or all of the elements that make up something. It's the most powerful component in relationships that provide spark. This is not scientifically detected, but you will know when it is there.

211. Use your God-given humor. You and your sphere of influence need it. It's been said *smart* people are humorous.

212. In relationships, people will trust you with the very best and the worst of them.

213. Deep relationship expresses dreams, fears, expectations, happiness, and disappointments.

214. Be real in meetings. Be the real you. Be the one your friends adore. Be this way all of the time, even in serious meetings.

215. Wear nice clothes. (They represent you.) Remember, people will respond to what they see in you.

216. Listen to a woman's feelings, not just her ideas. A wealth of knowledge relies on this gift. This certainly will help women that are strangers treat each other much better.

217. When unwanted and unethical things come to your mind, pray, "Lord, I cast this done in Jesus' name." For example, "I will not allow jealousy, envy, hatred, or any prejudices into my life in Jesus' name. I pray for blessing in their life, in Jesus' name."

218. When one says "Bill Gates," we immediately think of his company Microsoft. When people say your name, what will they immediately think of? You have a lifetime to correct, enhance and build your brand.

219. Never allow past experiences in life to be all you achieve. Your life is not over until you move on to heaven. I am really being

extremely positive here. Give people a philosophy of guaranteed success. This can't possibly happen without the Lord in your life.

220. Each morning you awake, forget yesterday, and choose to enjoy today. Expect good things to happen for you and others.

221. Try to bring joy to someone's life today.

222. Eat something good for you for breakfast. You will need the energy to keep you fueled until lunch.

223. Hug and kiss those you love before you leave each day. Hugs do wonders for emotional health and acceptance.

224. Each day, be the best person you can be. Be conscientious of this. The world will appreciate this.

225. Trying to be perfect in life can simply paralyze any person. Be careful. Allow yourself a break.

226. Bravery and masculine power is a vital source for men.

227. A man has a major part in making his wife happy, but he is not to be her sole source. He is not there to answer all of her questions, heal all of her wounds, fill the cup of her spirit, and make her whole. That's for her Creator. Stay in your lane. This is for women and men to know.

228. Demand respect; this is a healthy building block for humanity. When you don't, you will become unattractive.

229. The Bible contains thousands of progressive principles and promises for those that honor God.

230. The best way to draw people to you is to express self-confidence, be exciting, interested in many things, and acquire a certain independence.

231. Practice making people feel important and express great respect for them and *what they are saying.*

232. If you don't think you are important and valuable, no one will. People will treat you just like you treat yourself. You really need to take an annual checkup on how you treat yourself. Remember, one of the top three commandments is to love yourself. I hate to say this, but some people go a little overboard with this, and others treat themselves like stray dogs.

233. Never let your spouse be an object of ridicule or laughter around others.

234. Be *proactive* and not always reactive. Don't always let life determine your life.

235. Be excited about life! You are part of something absolutely filled with billions of miracles. Billions more happen each and every day.

236. Have a little fun each day, don't be shy about spending some time being silly. This, too, keeps you happy.

237. Become part of some organized team at your school or in the community. This experience will bless you in so many ways in your life.

238. As you begin to refine and define yourself, *the more you will love yourself.* Many don't love themselves because they have only been mainly exposed to the repercussions of their own sinful life.

239. Never make the wrong mistake about God; know and clearly understand He is *only* a loving Creator who definitely wants the best for you and who desires to have a relationship with you.

240. All discipline for a moment seems not to be joyful but sorrowful; yet to those who have learned from it, afterward will add to a fruitful future. After all, we all want to be corrected when we are completely wrong. No one in their right mind really wants to be wrong.

241. Mentors and counselors can enable many to have a more exciting and happy life. They are good and perfect gifts from above.

242. As you read the Bible daily, it will help keep you from succumbing to the pressures of what this world produces each day. Start with Psalms, Proverbs, and then the Gospels (Matthew, Mark, Luke, and John).

243. God has set His laws for all time and for all people. No hard-core special interest group or voting party will ever change it. Your arms are too short to box with God.

244. Invest in the life of your close friends, be a blessing to them and not a curse. As you get older in life, you will be so glad you nurtured these relationships. Stay very close to at least one or two.

245. Master the ability to forgive quickly. This will eliminate you are being held captive, and it will eliminate many sicknesses in your life. Make necessary adjustments with wrongdoers but always forgive whatever is done.

246. Always express gratitude to those that render kindness to you. Say *thank you* for every little thing they do for you. You will find as you grow older that little things are just as valuable as large things.

247. Say "I am sorry" when you have wronged someone. Don't substitute this action with flowers or anything material. You can, however, give these items to emphasize that you are very sorry. Don't let your being in the dog house be the only time you get flowers for your loved one.

248. Tell people that you love them often, especially your significant one and your children. Hug your children and always be the last to release the hug. Never give up on your children. Remember, they do not know as much as you.

249. Learn about the different personalities of mankind: sanguine, choleric, melancholic, and phlegmatic. This will help you

understand why people are talkative, quiet, energetic, and simply want to be alone often. They all are beautiful and very normal but need to be understood. If you don't understand their nature, you will certainly misunderstand them often and horribly misjudge them. For example, you never try to make your highly reserved phlegmatic child become a salsa teacher.

250. Be a person of great patience. People will love you for it.

251. In listening to others, never try to bring answers to all of their problems. Just being a sounding board sometimes is enough.

252. Be interested in other people's subjects even if it is not your cup of tea. If their subjects are important to them, allow them to be important to you.

253. If you have never been trained to be a father, mother, good citizen, or friend, you need to get books on the subject and go to some church to be trained. If you don't, how can you be knowledgeable and be able to master the responsibility? To become a winner in anything, you must get all the knowledge about it.

254. Foolishness is bound in the heart of people; they will need wisdom to succeed.

255. Don't ever completely blame others for the position in life that you are currently in, especially when you can decide right now to move forward with what you can do to excel in life.

256. Don't be one to put others down just to let your light shine.

257. Flattery is ineffective, but true compliments encourage people to progress in life.

258. The Word of God, which is the Bible, is proven to be an awesome and infallible place to start your life over with. It is the very best standard to judge and live your entire life by.

259. A great parent will encourage his children to have the right ethics, morals, and spiritual truths. Children will need more than a secular education to have a well-rounded and balanced life.

260. Do unto others as you would have them to do unto you.

261. If you are always looking down and frowning, people will avoid you.

262. Let your conversations be about others and not always about you.

263. At least introduce yourself to your neighbors; you will never know when you will need them.

264. "Thou shalt not bear false witness" (Exodus 20:16, KJV). Keep saying this about six times a day, and you will find yourself lying less and less. This is what's called "meditating on scriptures," and your heart and conduct will change in time.

265. Married couples will soon find that they will disagree and this could lead to them almost hating one another. But the thing they must remember is that they still love each other and realize it's just part of having a relationship that needs to be gently worked out. Someone must apologize first and begin to serve each other again.

266. To truly honor God is to love people.

267. Every city needs people of deep-rooted ethics and morals.

268. Don't try to put out every fire that springs up in your daily life. Overlook the small stuff and let God handle what you cannot.

269. Forgive quickly and focus more on the good and great things about people. Be known for being a person of courage, unconditional love, and wisdom.

270. To stop bad habits, replace them with good habits. The body will hate it but continue until you win. If you need the

assistance of spiritual deliverance, contact a full Gospel church that ministers spiritual warfare and personal deliverance.

271. Be kind to women, young men. Respect them and always honor them.

272. Respect all that are in authority. Talk to them the way you want to be talked to.

273. When you are upset, communicate when you calm down. Look people in the eyes and be firm when you must.

274. Respect yourself. People respect those that think highly of themselves. Beware, however, and don't think more highly of yourself than you ought.

275. Get as much secular education when you are young. When you are married with a full-time job and family, this will become a much greater challenge.

276. Learn all you can because when you are a little older, you will pay dearly for what you don't know.

277. Learn as much as you can about everything. You will pay for what you don't know eventually.

278. You may want to consider not taking part in body battered sports for too many years. You will pay physically later in life. What's the sense in having all that money and not being able to think or walk?

279. When a woman goes through her different cycles of life, she is extremely sensitive and different. Be a master of patience and just say okay, baby, everything is okay.

280. When a man is in a rut, he does not need a massive stream of complaints coming from anyone. Statements like "You can do it, baby, what can I do to assist you?" is what he needs. Tell him, "You are my strong honk; you and God will make things happen. No matter how long it takes and whatever condition we may face, I promise to be with you." This will give you the

key to his heart. He will never forget how you made him feel when he was going through life's tough challenges.

281. A woman needs security, love, and to feel special.

282. A man is to be respected, encouraged, and loved adequately.

283. Let the world know that you love one another.

284. Don't drive too close to others. Stay one car link every ten miles per hour. This will give plenty of time to stop if something happens.

285. Never park right beside a van at night. Never walk in unfamiliar areas at night or early in the morning.

286. Keep your clothes, car, and house clean. It makes you feel better. A cluttered home is a nest for confusion.

287. Get a home warranty for all of your appliances; it saves a lot of money when they are worn out.

288. When you and your significant one have knock-down drag-outs or a heated discussion, don't go running into other arms. Take a break and go riding and listen to some music that makes you happy. Go back and just be quiet until the storm dissipates. You might have to say "I'm sorry" even when you are not wrong. Or you can just say, "Baby, I was not wrong with this, as you know, but I am sorry all this happened because I miss our love and peace." There will be times when your pride doesn't matter; it's the investment you have in relationships that matter. You never want to lose your relationships if you don't have to.

289. Grass will always look greener on the other side. Remember, they are always looking their best around you. You really don't know them when they are not presenting their best. Your grass would be greener if you just water it.

290. If you know nothing about cars, have your oil, water, and tires checked every quarter by someone you trust. This will save you lots of money and pain.

291. Never try to make a person be your friend. There are those that would love to; give them the chance. Beautiful, high profile, and popular friends won't matter later in life. If they like you and are good to you, invite them to be your friend now.

292. Stay away from lots of food that fill your arteries with cholesterol. This will cause heart disease, diabetes, and other sicknesses later in life. Too much pork, cheese, and burgers will catch up with you.

293. It is, however, better to eat a burger with a friend than eat a steak with someone that will do you no good.

294. Give people their compliments and flowers now. Many are gone because we never tell people how we feel about them. Again reveal your whole heart to those you love; it will bless you in the long run.

295. When mowing your lawn, wear eye protection. Also, wear a dust mask. You may be allergic to the grass. Never mow the lawn when it is too hot outside. Wait until it is cooler.

296. If you are too heavy, don't get on a ladder. If you are not a professional in cutting trees or doing work on the roof, leave it alone!

297. Never drive intoxicated. This can happen with dope, alcohol, or prescription drugs. You will be ticketed for the use of either.

298. Relinquish being part of a gang and selling drugs. You will place your entire family in great danger.

299. Be known for being a gentleman. There are many men but very few gentlemen. Be known as being a graceful lady. There are many women but very few ladies.

300. Speak only about positive things when you are dining with others.

301. If you don't have good ideas, don't complain about the ideas of others.

302. Quit assuming the worse about people. Be sure about what you think of others.

303. If you have recently come out of a bad relationship, never run to another until your heart is healed. You must find out what you may have done wrong as well. Your negative baggage can further injure you and others.

304. Beauty and a person's quality come from within. Often you will meet people that are beautiful or handsome on the outside but are a mess on the inside.

305. Make money, but be a person of integrity and character. This will bring peace and joy to your life. People will love and honor you for it.

306. Be spontaneous. This will bring excitement to your life. Don't make people have to plan everything with you. Take well-calculated risks.

307. Success is the sum of doing and being all that you were placed here to do or be.

308. Leave your world around you a better place.

309. Be responsible, proactive, persistent, resilient, and considerate.

310. Encourage your children to start working soon in life. When they have to work for money, they will then understand the true value of money.

311. Compliment all small and great accomplishments of your children. This will help their esteem and propel them to greater levels in life.

312. When you are offended, get the person by themselves and tell them that they hurt you. Many times people don't know unless you make them aware of their error. You have to love yourself enough to do this. People will also respect you more.

313. Homeowners, many times it is not good to let relatives rent from you, especially if they are known for not paying their bills.

314. Go to bed early during the week so you can be a good employee the next day at work. You *promised* to be an asset. Keep your word. Don't let your friends keep you out at all times at night. Stay off the phone at work.

315. Don't purchase something new because your friend does it. Sometimes they will encourage you to do it because the misery of too much debt loves company.

316. Don't misuse or hate people because your friend doesn't like them. You are better than that.

317. When greeting people, genuinely tell them it is good to see them.

318. Put your full confidence only in God and not man. Man is fallible; remember this. They are not perfect, and they are not omnipotent.

319. Enjoy the gifts and talents of others. Give them their props. Letting jealousy rule in your life will make you an unlikely candidate for a friend.

320. When out shopping and people are trying to rush you, stop them and tell them you want to go home and think about this purchase.

321. People generally never forget when you do them wrong. Be kind to all people, large, small, rich, poor, white, or black. Again, apologize when you are wrong. You will have to at times because you are not perfect. People will forgive you, and they will appreciate you for humbling yourself.

322. Exercise also causes endorphins to be released in your brain. This produces happy feelings and energy and eliminates depression.

323. Go get checkups from the doctor. They will save you lots of pain. Many people don't go because they are afraid that doctors will

find something wrong. This is foolishness. Yes, hold physicians accountable and appreciate them for doing a good job, but never ignore this great benefit to society. People have died early because they refused regular checkups, and then at the funeral, some ignorant person blamed God for taking them.

324. Make yourself a major asset to the company you work for. Never join with hating the supervisor for holding you accountable for doing your job.

325. Go to work with the right attitude. No one has to give you anything. No one owes you anything. When you work hard, you will reap the rewards.

326. When you are invited to a meeting, bring ideas that could possibly help the vision of your company.

327. Be a person of excellence. Whatever your profession is, do it well. People cannot ignore excellence. They will travel unlimited miles for your product.

328. Be a team player. The light does not always have to shine on you. Compliment others when they have good ideas. Human nature has the ability to not accept the good in others.

329. Supervisors and managers, remember to be fair and treat employees with respect. Remember, God is watching you. The people that you climb on to reach the top will be those you will need to help keep you there.

330. When you don't have anything good to say, say nothing.

331. Give every child a chance to excel in life. This means accepting them and helping them because so many have experienced great dysfunction and inadequate support. It is easy to play the blame game for the ills of society, but please remember you can help change a lot using this wisdom.

332. Controlling a person's will is wrong. Make a person love you only by the loving things you do and say.

333. If you want to have something worth listening to, start to read, read, and read. Surf the internet. Keep up with current events. Read magazines. Go to the library. Go to church.

334. Develop a family photo tree for your children.

335. Focus more on the favorite qualities of others and your mate.

336. As you move forward with your dreams, learn from seasons of interruptions. Don't allow them to stop you. You might have to shed some tears, and that's okay. Nevertheless, stay resilient.

337. Watch your children closely and lead them in the direction of their passions and their obvious giftings.

338. The principles in the Bible can solve every problem in the entire world.

339. Love preserves the family.

340. To be strengthened is to surround yourself with words that strengthen you.

341. If you change what people know, you can change what they do. We are our brother's keeper. Sometimes, people need a little help to get out of a rut. It's said that people in so-called third-world countries only need medical help, clean water, education, and be shown how to produce agriculture, and they will be fine.

342. Watch it; you have what you say. Here's a quick example: say, "I'm sleepy" fifty times and see what happens. You will tend to get sleepy.

343. Kindness and love will always help with emotional healing.

344. Mothers, don't allow your little boys to wear your shoes or put on your attire and lipstick. This will deceive him and destroy his masculinity.

345. When you are married, you vow not to live a single life anymore. You owe this to your spouse to let them know where you are, at least most of the time. Call when you have to work late.

346. When you go on an interview, dress very well, have your research done concerning the company and be ready to ask questions about the future goals of the company.

347. Always be optimistic, faithful, and continue to learn and grow. The day you stop learning is the day the world will leave you, and you fall behind.

348. Be careful when using credit cards. It will take you years to pay them off. The debt will make you miserable. Save and buy what you want with cash.

349. Many times, you can be a homeowner with the same amount of money that you rent or lease. You must, however, pay your bills on time, so your credit can be good. This will qualify you to buy a house.

350. The chamber of commerce is also mainly responsible for bringing businesses to your city.

351. We go to God in prayer because wise people know that spiritual wisdom produces glory, honor, and good.

352. God is preparing people for greatness by the church.

353. When we love one another, we help prevent self-destruction.

354. Socialism is a total government takeover. One step away from communism.

355. Every major city has its coven of witches, underground groups that will be sent to oppose the work of God. Through prayer, we are to cast out those evil spirits, release the fire of God upon them, the judgment of God, and the sword of the Lord, in Jesus' name.

356. Connecting with God and His plan for you keeps life flowing into our lives, releases significance, brings joy into what you do, recharges our spirits and souls, and eliminates repetitiveness, boredom, emptiness, and a life of no meaning.

357. God formed us like Him, we are special to Him, and He gave us intelligence.

358. No matter what work you do, you should always have loving God and caring for people be the center of it.

359. Caring means developing people professionally, personally, and spiritually.

360. To quit a bad habit will call for some pain to be attached and associated with it. Disciplining yourself is painful in some aspects. Give a person at least sixty days to change any bad habit. They need that much grace. After a worse day of developing a new discipline, you will finally win.

361. When human relations (soft training) is invested, many times productivity will double in any company.

362. Life becomes dull when you become reactive instead of proactive.

363. Vocation is comprised of several occupations: job, business, church, hobbies, family, etc.

364. A CEO of any corporation (profit or nonprofit) needs leaders that are not afraid to take risks, and they must be those to take initiative.

365. Get a public insurance adjuster when you have to deal with insurance companies as a result of a fire, weather catastrophe, etc. You will need a person that understands that business to get from the insurance companies what you have paid for and now deserve.

366. People don't get married to get a divorce. You both must get knowledge, wisdom, and divine understanding to be able to stay together and receive all that's needed to live together successfully. All that you need can be provided at a good Word or Bible-teaching church.

367. Success is the progressive realization and internalization of what you were meant to do and be. You can get a start to realizing all this through a good church.

368. Good health will require drinking plenty of water and not soft drinks every day.

369. You make your life significant when you change the world.

370. Keep up with current events and technology. Don't get left behind. As it relates to the news media sources, don't rely on one particular one all the time. Find a couple that carries mostly true, happy, and positive stories.

371. Discipline is conscientiously controlling your life and not allowing life to control you.

372. Proactive people are victors, and reactive people are victims.

373. Fulfillment begins when life is meaningful.

374. Using these wisdoms guarantee a pattern of success and excellence.

375. The main problem with crime is people need a change of heart; only God and the Bible provide that. You can try to continue to legislate this and provide programs and money all you want to. You will still have a heart that needs to be changed. Yes, many will need financial and other support, but the heart must be dealt with immediately.

376. Blessed is the nation whose God is the Lord. This goes for an individual as well (Psalm 33:12).

377. Demand respect; it's a fundamental building block of all healthy connections.

378. You can't please everyone; use wisdom with this. You and your family must be first. Also, accept the fact that not everyone will like you.

379. Marriage is tough sometimes, but stay with it; the fire of love will make things better when it's all done. Tough seasons never last forever. Stay together.

380. You will never always feel in love; never let your feelings always lead you. The flames of love can always be rekindled.

381. Give a man space and time to be alone sometimes or be with other men. He also needs time to refocus and gather himself.

382. No matter what you do, men, always let your woman know she is more valuable than anything, and I mean anything. She needs to know this very, very often. Not only say this but prove it.

383. Do something each day to prove that you love your spouse. As they notice this, they should do the same. This keeps romance and intimacy alive.

384. Married couples never need to say the word "divorce," ever.

385. Practice always being kind, grateful, respectful, and appreciative to your spouse and never taking them for granted.

386. The weakness of your spouse is what God uses many times to develop your character.

387. You are better than what you are choosing to do that is wrong. Get around different people, change your environment, and start attending church, community centers, and wherever positive people are.

388. It will never matter what background you came from; God will assist you in every way to become successful. Just trust and obey Him.

389. Generally, people will not ever quit a job without one being readily available.

390. Never steal from anyone.

391. Always prove to be a trusted friend.

392. Go to bed at night and get a good night's sleep. Help maintain and produce your optimum.

393. Never be a person that parties *all* the time. That's just not wise. There is a time for everything. There is a time for business and a time for playing.

394. Always make time for your spouse and your children. Making money is not everything your family needs. Use wisdom. For those whose dream has always been to reach the top of the corporate ladder, if you have a family, stay there just for a moment and get back to serving your family adequately.

395. You can never spoil your children with too much love and hugs. You spoil them with too many material things instead of your presence in their lives. They need and want your time instead of your money.

396. The more you give, the more you love. Both words have very similar ancient Hebrew directives.

397. You feel loving when you love.

398. You generally fall in love with the good that people do for you.

399. When you go out, you may want to join to help a friend in distress.

400. Apply goodness to people by encouragement based on the things they have shared with you or the things that you have picked up.

401. Everyone has something to live for. Everyone has a God-predestined purpose and meaning. Receiving Christ as your Savior will help lead the way.

402. Just begin to love people, and you will begin a life of love. Yes, you can love without even knowing a person. You can affirm and love their commitments to goodness and seeking God. We love because God commanded us to. We may not like a person's evil ways, but we are to love.

403. Infatuation is thinking a person is perfect and you don't even know them. It feels like love.

404. Love is when you appreciate the virtues of another person and you identify with them.

405. Men and women are different. We are to be profoundly aware of this, allow them to be who they are, benefit from them, celebrate them and treasure the differences. We error when we think they should be like us. Many times we conclude by thinking they are strange and therefore unimportant and impermissible.

406. If you are ready to get married, it means you are ready to take responsibility for a wife and a family.

407. The emotional foundation of love is trust. Do you trust them completely? Be honest and ask yourself this before you get married.

408. To love your mate is to master: touch, gifts, service, quality time, words of affirmation, and taking care of each other's needs.

409. Learn to appreciate and savor the wonderful things in life. From people to food, from nature to a smile.

410. The most important source of happiness is the person close to you; appreciate them, savor and cherish the time you spend together.

411. Whenever a crisis comes, consider each one as another challenge that will make you better and smarter.

412. Try not to be predictable and too routine.

413. He who *conceals an offense* promotes *love*. In other words, don't be too sensitive.

414. A principle of self-control is to control the tongue. We don't have to speak the first word that comes to our mind.

415. He that is quick-tempered does stupid things, and one who does vile things is hated. People with good sense are slow to anger, and it is their glory to overlook an offense.

416. When you are training anyone, you are asking them to give you their heart and a commitment of their will, intellect, and emotions. This commitment is a necessary part of a real education.

417. Don't train up a child in the way they want to go; this includes all of their selfish desires (spoiling), and surely when they get old, they may not depart from it. Be your child's parent and not their running buddy.

418. The relationship of the children with their parents is a vital indicator of the family's health.

419. Anger can be a seed, and hatred will become the tree.

420. Quarrels and nagging are mechanisms by which people attempt to address a problem. Two sorts of quarrelsome people, one that has a legit issue and someone that just quarrels all the time. This will bring dysfunction. Some dysfunction is minor and can be overlooked, but not abuse, poor child-raising, neglect, adultery, etc.

421. Family can be a blessing if people have the right attitude and things are properly understood.

422. Don't plain embarrass yourself by saying things that are uninformed or just plain wrong. It's okay not to know something about every subject.

423. The richest person in the world is a person that is completely satisfied with your lot and what you have. God provides so very much for us to enjoy, but He is not responsible for us choosing to enjoy them. Therefore in your current level of prosperity, thank God for His favor, His blessings, and be established as a strong mountain.

424. Material things are simply to be used as tools and not to become trophies of what we are solely here to accomplish. We are here to take responsibility for this world via the generation we live in. Hence, the greatest opportunity in life is to serve others; a clear avenue to be joyful; spreading good and joy to all people. To become happy is to make others happy, to be honored to honor others. Christianity is an exceptional system for this type of living, built upon a relationship with God through Christ, strengthened upon obligations and many wisdoms. For example, one who is strong is one that can overcome his own inclinations and temptations; one who is wise is one that can learn from everyone.

425. Chase after God's wisdom because its truth will bring the greatest love, pleasures, meaning, value, preparation, hope, and stability into your life.

426. Your art, your self-actualization in life, will identify who we really are and will send a distinct message to all, even to your beloved heavenly Father. Be sincere, be genuine.

427. The truth of God stands against all opposition and proves to be absolute and victorious every time.

428. People involved in knowing the knowledge of good and evil often get confused and end up not knowing what is good and what is evil.

429. Intelligence is expressed in ultimately loving yourself. You love yourself when you desire to be successful. Success is the progressive realization and internalization of what you were meant to do and be.

430. You and I are to be one with things that make life significant as you do things to change the world.

431. Make sure your kids turn out hard-working, productive, and great citizens.

432. Make your life fulfilling and rich. Work hard but be safe.

433. The Bible is the most priceless possession of the human race. This is why Satan, in all of his power, tries to keep you away from it.

434. Growth is also a by-product of excellent service. Albert Einstein asked the question, "Why are we here?" To serve others. It's a fact that when we stop serving others, by the third month, we will become completely irritated. People who succeed make themselves more valuable as service than others. Go the extra mile in service.

435. Give people more than they expect. This can also be a great contribution to our society.

436. When you are responsible for anything, make sure you have a plan A and a plan B.

437. You will never get rich or prosperous if you don't enrich others' lives and cause others to prosper.

438. As you grow in value as a person, you receive the income you seek.

439. If we dwell on and expect failure, then that's exactly what will occur in our lives.

440. When life gets rough, stay focused. Weeping may endure for a night, but joy comes in the morning.

441. Search for the benefits that come from failure, defeat, and adversity. Learn from those unfortunate instances.

442. Keep a right mental attitude with a definite purpose with full belief in the soundness of that purpose.

443. You need to set goals in your life as to where you are going and what you're trying to accomplish. Write it down so you can see it every day.

444. Don't be fooled; people have troubles, fears, and worries, and they need Jesus. How can they not when they were born in sin, spiritually blind, have no true peace, and are inherently evil?

445. Sickness came from Satan, and it is a curse. Jesus redeemed us and brought us back from the curse.

446. Without a doubt, this is your season to overcome and excel. You can do this!

447. Meekness is also the amazing strength of a man and his boldness under control.

448. God would not give you a spouse to live a single life.

449. God has chosen the weak things of the world to shame the things which are mighty.

450. Some of the greatest workplaces are those that impact laws, values, and public opinions.

451. What wards off loneliness? When you bring your life to church, bring your heart, mind, and ears to seek the preached Word of God. Receive the corporate anointing, participate in praise and worship, fellowship, receive divine care, the love of God, the presence and blessing, the closeness of God, plus the family of God with all of their hugs. This will refresh your mind, bless your heart, your navel, your feet, and your spirit, rejuvenate your body and soul, and restore hope and excitement in your life.

452. God can erase uncontrollable anger, wounded hearts, and fears and help change those that perpetrate it. People need freedom, preservation, safety, purging, honor, fruitfulness, meeting, guidance, victory, faith, and godly wisdom that will last forever.

453. True intimacy also derives from loving God with all of your heart, soul, mind, and strength, which is the first and greatest Commandment. How ironic is that?

454. True recovery also requires quietness, diet, and rest.

455. When your character is developed, you will not have to worry about being ashamed.

456. The world is the ultimate channel by which God displays His miracles.

457. The place of your greatest agony can also become the place where your greatest victory comes from.

458. Don't try to stop all your traditions; just let your unity and your times of celebration include God.

459. When you are good to people, you set yourself and favorable positions.

460. Maturity and growth also come after challenges, opposition, problems, and issues. Attack and solve them all.

461. One that is mature and mighty is one that overcomes his inclinations.

462. One who is wise is one who learns from everyone.

463. Aim at building deep and lasting relationships. This may mean don't be so quick to kick the relationship to the curb when you are offended. Remember, most of us invest everything and years in relationships. Give them the opportunity to be restored if you can.

464. Appreciation of wisdom and understanding is what produces excellence.

465. Know that you are making a difference. The world needs you.

466. One thing I heard about our latest generation is that they are smart as can be, but they lack being part of things that help make the world better, and they invest in their life without a picture of life's ultimate purpose and cause.

467. Vocation is comprised of several occupations, jobs, churches, businesses, hobbies, family, etc. We all have a call to fulfill this, being our very best in every area of it.

468. Caring for others equals developing people professionally, personally, and spiritually.

469. Value yourself by being your very best professionally and personally. It also includes speaking up and stepping up.

470. Intelligence makes your life meaningful. Intelligence is being wise, understanding, and smart.

471. People that don't quit stick to goals and disciplines, even when it hurts. They are people that accomplish things. Using this wisdom will bring a pattern of success.

472. Be responsible for your attitude, mistakes, beliefs, and commitments. Make appropriate changes.

473. Have fun but don't live completely haphazardly.

474. Never disregard lessons of history. History has taught us a lot.

475. Stop and choose to be happy. Every day, arise and choose to be happy no matter what happens.

476. Never allow familiarity to reduce the value of those precious people around you. Celebrate them more.

477. Wise men were those who came to see the baby Jesus.

478. True friendship is based upon love. It's based upon those that are free from greed, lust, and violence. They agree upon subjects that bring goodwill towards one another. They only do well to one another. Their mutual loyalty brings only good stability and permanence to the relationship.

479. It's said that the golden rule of a friend was to put himself on the same level as his friend. Friendship pertains to having a special interest in someone. It refers to being loving, kind, devoted, dear, intimate, and of a close association with you. It's having a partner kind of spirit, one that is good to you and for you.

480. Bravery and masculine power are vital sources for men.

481. The best way to pull others to you is to express self-confidence, excitement, interest in many things, certain independence, and a certain ability to go unconnected with others until the end if it is something God requires.

482. If you don't think you are valuable, no one will.

483. Never let your best friend or your spouse be an object of ridicule or laughter around others.

484. Be proactive and don't let life determine your life.

485. Have a little fun each day, a time of silliness and happiness.

486. Prophecy should be only edification, exhortation, and comfort to your ears.

487. Everyone needs to be heard, felt, and understood.

488. Proverbs 3:8 (AMP) says (Bible wisdom) literally, "It will be health to your body [your marrow, your nerves, your sinews, your muscles—all your inner parts] And refreshment (physical well-being) to your bones. from God will bring health to our nerves and moisten our bones."

489. We are to root out, throw down, pulldown, plant, build, occupy, possess, invade, and concur.

490. Sexual misconduct makes you lose your honor.

491. Obedience is a form of safety and protection. Therefore laws received have the ability and power to protect you.

492. Fear is a choice; you can focus on it or not.

493. Principles and truths help us grow, build, and develop character.

494. Everyone was created to solve a problem. You are a reward to somebody (1 Corinthians 2:9).

495. What you hate is a clue to what you are here to correct.

496. What you love is also a clue to the gifts, talents, skills, and wisdom that you have.

497. Know that sometimes life is filled with interruptions. Tend to them and get back refocused immediately. They come to distract.

498. Writing a disclaimer protects you as a business owner.

499. Watch your thoughts because they quickly become words, words become actions, actions become habits, habits become character, character becomes your future, and your future will become your destiny. (Watch what you listen to, too.)

500. God says in Job 36:11 (ESV), "If they listen and serve him, they complete their days in prosperity, and their years in pleasantness."

501. Wisdom is the greatest gift you can give anyone. It outweighs all gold and silver.

502. Prophets have these gifts: discerning of spirit, word of knowledge, and words of wisdom.

503. Honor and love people for the sheer joy of it, and it will enhance your life.

504. There is a war going on for the soul of America.

505. Gifts of all kinds nourish relationships.

506. You need to be doing something that you are passionate about.

507. Don't be focused wholly on your hourly wage; help your employer sell his business.

508. Long-scale righteousness builds wealth.

509. Nothing blesses a man more than knowing that a woman cares for him.

510. Passion is generated when one shows that they truly care for you. Also, show appreciation. Also, declare your affections as soon as you feel them.

511. There is magic in the words "I love you." Friends and family will love you for saying it. Children respond to it.

512. Best relationships are built only by many small acts of love and kindness.

513. Highlight people that take their valuable time to make you feel good and make you enjoy moments of happiness.

514. Declare thousands of tiny statements of love.

515. Celebrations (anniversaries, etc.) are very important in all cultures. Make sure you acknowledge them.

516. The test of a good person is easily detected in how they treat the little people. Also, watch how people treat their parents, especially their mother.

517. A lover allows their beloved to be free and have space when needed.

518. Nothing is ever as bad as it first appears.

519. Patience will make deception reveal itself.

520. You never reach the palace talking like a peasant.

521. What you will make happen for others, God will make happen for you.

522. Your divine assignments in life are your destiny.

523. Persecution is part of success. You will be the object of jealousy.

524. God saved us to be our God.

525. It's said that Congress printed the first Bibles for schools.

526. Lots of wrongdoing produces mental distress; that's why people need peace.

527. Meekness is humility, maturity, self-control, wisdom, strength, and discipline.

528. People mainly want pleasure, power, prestige, position, and prosperity.

529. One of our greatest blessings is to have a character flaw revealed to us and have a way to correct it. Allow people to correct you. Don't have people afraid to correct you. This could save you a lot of headaches.

530. In a deceived, insecure and confused world, Christianity is a stabilizing force and a light.

531. We must never live according to our feeling and fears. Live by principles and truths.

532. Whenever someone controls your joy and happiness, it's called idolatry.

533. Loving your spouse unconditionally will save your marriage.

534. You must think of ways and things to do to show kindness.

535. Take care of yourself. Grow up and do the things that keep you healthy instead of getting sick or getting hurt by simply being unsafe and clumsy. This places needless heartache on your family and your employers. Pay attention and be responsible. Abide by the rules or safety and law. When you have a little discomfort or pain, grow up and quit being a big baby and a nuisance to everyone you know. This is also being tagged as being high maintenance. By the way, let people talk to you like you are an adult. People hate having to walk on eggshells when they are around immature and supersensitive people. Toughen up!

536. Stop being mean when you are hungry, tired, or have not had your coffee. That is not an excuse for being rude and, many times, verbally abusive. Control yourself.

537. Just because you have money, own the company, or your folks are rich does not give you the right to treat people as if they are less than you.

538. The days are completely over when it comes to race jokes or being racist. Those days are dead and buried!

539. You can enjoy the greatness of the opposite sex if you can just stop lusting on them.

540. To hold a grudge is human but to forgive is divine.

541. Bitterness and unforgiveness will also destroy your joy and peace of mind. As a matter of fact, many people are sick and in the hospital now because of worry or bitterness and unforgiveness.

542. Love endures long and is patient and kind. It is never envious or boils over with jealousy. Love is not boastful or prideful. Love does not insist on its own rights or its own way but is not self-seeking. Love is not touchy or fretful or resentful; it takes no account of the evil done to it, and it pays no attention to a suffered wrong. Love does not rejoice in injustice or unrighteousness but rejoices when right and truth prevail. Love bears up under anything and everything that comes. Love is ever ready to believe the best of every person, love's hopes are fadeless under all circumstances, and it endures everything without weakening. Love never fails, never fades out, or comes to an end.

543. The purpose of your neighbor is to love your neighbor.

544. Are you part of the problem in your city or part of the solution? We all have the responsibility of being great citizens of any city or country that we are part of. We have the responsibility of making people feel safe, accepted, loved, and appreciated.

545. If you have a problem with releasing bitterness or unforgiveness, ask God to help you to give you the strength to do it.

546. Forgiveness does not mean that a person should not have to earn your trust again. Forgiveness does not mean that when people cause major issues, they shouldn't pay the penalty of the law of the land.

547. The Greek has four words that describe love: "Eros," a physical attraction, or sexual type of love. "Phileo" is love and affection between friends. "Storge," love and affection between family members, and "Agape," the ultimate God kind of love. This is the highest form of love. This love gives and expects nothing in return. This love realizes the complete value of others. It's the unconditional acceptance of other people and the active seeking of their highest good. It's the exercise of choice to love rather than to hate. This love is action instead of complacency.

548. The single biggest reason for many people's faith not working and for their prayers not being answered is the lack of love, Agape love, and practicing this love in their life.

549. After praying for deliverance for other people; pray against sabotage, backlash, retaliation, and revenge for yourself; pray this for yourself.

550. Many times, people can be healed of sicknesses if they ask God to forgive them for doing other people wrong. Asking people to forgive you will also help with this.

551. Have you ever heard that "sticks and stones may break my bones, but words will never hurt me?" That is not true; sticks and stones will break bones, and words will hurt and injure forever. Be very careful what you say to people.

552. We must stay principled people. People that live by success principles.

553. Church is a place to go and a way of living in relationship with God and others in His family.

554. Water baptism is a sign of your faith in Christ; it is obedience to God's Word, it is a sign of us publicly turning our backs on

a sinful life, and it's a declaration that we are against all evil forces. It is a sign of us being connected with God and taking on the name of Christ. It is the cleansing of the heart and the conscious. People can get water baptized as often as they like. Many get baptized as a sign that they are starting life all over. This is wonderful and acceptable to your Creator.

555. Being defensive all the time never produces ultimate victory in life. You must be a person of proactivity. Make things happen, and you can do this. If you want help from God, and you will need his help, humble yourself and ask for Him to help you. You can start by going to church and being part of the great family of God.

556. No one was meant to be alone. God created you and me to be part of His family. His family is the church. Many of you need to quit running from God. He is not a God that is trying to stop you from having fun. He just wants you to have fun the right way. What's the matter with that?

557. Many people don't know that dancing in the church is a type of intercession or prayer that sets people free from bondages. When you see people running in the church, that's also prophetic; it's a type of running Satan out of your life.

558. Five percent of the people of the world own most of the wealth. The cause of the great suffering in the world is not because of God; it's because of man's greed.

559. No matter what you've heard, God does not go around killing folks and murdering people. He does not cause people to get hurt or make people sick to teach them a lesson. He is a God that gives life and love. The devil is the one that steals, kills, and destroys, according to the Bible (John 10:10). He is the one behind people making the decisions to hurt other folks, drive drunk and do things that cause death. He has been the one the whole time. He uses people to skillfully twist the blame, so people blame God in some way. He has been the one that

has successfully stopped you and many others from attending God's church. The ark of truth and the true pillow of faith.

560. When you love, you heal and bless the souls of others.

561. We must not fear the battles of the promised land. Remember, God is with us.

562. We all need to feel needed; therefore, find your purpose in God. The church can help you with this.

563. There are many hindrances in life but beware specifically of fear of man, failure, and rejection. Beware of excuses, isolation, individualism, spectatorship, and consumerism. You must overcome these.

564. Be optimistic, enthusiastic, and consistent and continue to grow.

565. Be involved in the community. Make sure you vote. Nonvoters have no right to complain.

566. The eyes are the window of the soul.

567. Beware of the following: handwriting analysis, tarot cards, Ouija boards, séances, astrology, star worship, mind control, astral projection, reincarnation, witchcraft, sorcery, satanism, reading horoscopes, tea leaf reading, gazing into a crystal ball, Dungeons & Dragons, many hypnoses, and all of their associations.

568. Be very careful about the songs that you listen to. Many of them have lyrics that are completely devastating to your life. Therefore, only listen to music that has lyrics that are encouraging and that are a blessing to your life. Listen to nothing that has vulgar lyrics demeaning people, especially women. Also, free your mind from songs that encourage you to do wrong.

569. Gambling casinos and other gambling organizations want 100 percent of your money. We all have seen this as great entertainment, but how entertaining is it when you lose all your money, lose your job, lose your family, end up on drugs,

and are completely destroyed. God only wants 10 percent, and He blesses the 90 percent.

570. Ungodly traditions of men have made the Word of God have no effect.

571. The kingdom of God is God's way of doing things, it's His rule, and it's His plans on the earth.

572. There are approximately two billion dollars spent yearly on advertisements in certain communities. Start using your finances wisely. Act like you are used to having things and money. Let's stop being bamboozled, hoodwinked, and used.

573. The church is the only place that teaches the correct nature of God and about divine interventions. Beware of any organization that tries to reinvent Christ, the Bible, and the church.

574. Jesus is a gift to the world, and the Holy Spirit is a gift to the church.

575. Ladies, men are task-oriented people; they are always trying to achieve and supply answers. Although brothers, women need us to just listen and be a sounding board sometimes.

576. All witchcraft is mostly about words; they know how the system of words works, and they know the power of words.

577. The Bible says a just man falleth seven times and rises up again.

578. To wait for God to answer your prayers entails ultimate trust in Him, not becoming impatient when His timetable for your final answers differs from yours. This is maturity.

579. People that look for deeper relationships look for new ways to do it.

580. The absence of a functioning father in the home hinders the balance, ideas, perception, behavior, and feelings of his children.

581. Many of the problems with women in society stem from men not leading correctly.

582. Unfortunately, many men sacrifice value systems for the thrill of the moment and won't discipline themselves.

583. If your wife has gone through abuse, tragedies, etc., you must not expect her to be superwoman until she is healed. When she needs help in simple matters, help her instead of insinuating she is a continual problem.

584. God gives you a spouse to help you, help them unload their baggage. God gave you them because He knew that you could be the one to help them with their weaknesses, their embarrassments, their shortcomings, and their fears. You are the one; do your job and show your love.

585. Call those things that be not as though they were. Call your spouse what you see them be. God already sees them that way.

586. It is male to conquer and female to nurture.

587. Don't get lost in ego and personal acquisition. Don't reduce yourself to sperm and cash.

588. Married couples, when going through tough times in your marriage, do not use other people for immediate gratification just because of what you're going through. Two wrongs never make a right. This, too, will pass.

589. Anger is really fear, defensiveness, maturity, and hurt, posing as something that seems strong instead of using vulnerability strength.

590. When you come home and yell at your family, you destroy the very foundation of joy that is established in your life. How smart is that?

591. Uninvolvement with your family is not good. Come out of your bedrooms and be part of the family's fellowship times. This goes for everyone in the family. If you don't, you will regret it as you grow older.

592. Many criticize those that are homeless and those that are addicted to alcohol and drugs. But have you really wondered why people are in the predicament that they're in?

593. Brothers, you don't need to shack or run from one woman to the next; what you really need is purpose, direction, and belonging.

594. Tough times, in many cases, can be the glue that makes the relationship better.

595. Make sure you enjoy the elders in the family, especially grandparents. You will miss them so very much once they go to heaven.

596. Ninety-nine percent of the criminals in prison have never known the meaning of empathy. This is why it's so easy for them to hurt people. (Make sure you realize and value what others feel.)

597. If you didn't grow up with a father, God will prove to be the greatest Father you could ever have. Give Him a chance.

598. Quit judging other people because you cannot completely understand them anyway; it's impossible. Your own judgments towards others can keep your heart in bondage.

599. Beauty is the harmony of all its parts. It is an exquisite combination of form, line, and color. It is the complex order present in the works of art and architecture. Scientists agree that nothing beautiful comes without the brilliance of a creator, God.

600. God is supreme intellect.

601. Don't take life so seriously; laugh, use your humor, enjoy yourself, and let the child in you play sometimes. Don't become a bore.

602. The glory of a man is his wife.

603. God thought of you first, then He created you.

604. A man needs an attractive wife. It is an emotional need of a woman to look good.

605. Don't try to pray people's faith where it is not. Find out what they want to pray about and then pray what they desire.

606. Be growth-minded; take every opportunity to grow. Most people don't want to learn or change because they feel like they are too exhausted, they dread the fear of the unknown, they think it's too hard to change, and they are concerned about what other people think. Get over it all. Take charge of your life! When you do, it's promised to be a phenomenal blessing.

607. If you want to lift more mental weight, you will be alright. Stretch yourself a little.

608. Fear will tell you over and over that you shouldn't even try. Don't let it continue to prevail in your life. To keep expecting something different and doing the same thing is extremely disheartening.

609. To change, you never have to worry about your age, you're never too old, you're good enough to do it, it is not harder than you thought, you don't have to have a perfect background, it's never too late, and nothing you have done will be used to stop you.

610. As a relates to friendship, awesome loyalty is required. It is work!

611. If you're going to be a part of a very intimate relationship, you must, and I repeat, you must be a person that shows affection. Affection is showing a person with all of your heart that you like them, that you love them, that you care for them, and that they are very special to you. Therefore, don't hold back on hugging them, kissing them, holding their hands, looking into their eyes, and doing things that really show them that the deepness of your heart is always open to them. Most people are very short on affection. Some are even embarrassed to show it in public. We have to change this quickly because without it, the relationship spirals.

612. If you want affection, you must show affection. You reap what you sow. You sow lots of affection; then you will reap lots of affection. In fact, married people have a contract before the living God to promise a life filled with affection for their spouse. Many have not received affection since their honeymoon. This is a sin and a shame.

613. People love it when we do things that give them little moments of happiness. But always notice when people do these things for you. Do not overlook them. Make sure you appreciate it, enjoy it, show gratitude, and reciprocate, reciprocate, reciprocate. This is actually heaven on earth. Don't lose this good thing. It takes years to find people of this caliber.

614. Couples, especially married couples, really need something that they can do together. This might mean volunteering in the community, or definitely, it could be being part of a ministry in the church to serve and work together.

615. You and I have the awesome opportunity to create the relationships we so deeply deserve.

616. Ladies, men are encouraged when they know that they can make you happy. Make sure you tell them everything that they do that makes you happy and that makes you feel good.

617. Opening your heart would certainly help you in the area of receiving and giving love.

618. The reason we need to know everything there is to know about the opposite sex is because men and women communicate differently, they think differently, they feel differently, they react differently, they respond differently, they love differently, they need differently, and they appreciate differently; therefore they need different nourishment and complete understanding to be able to be completely appreciated and satisfied.

619. Love should not ever hurt. If you notice that the one you love is hurting and unhappy, there must be something wrong with what you are doing; find out and fix it immediately.

620. Teach your children early in life about this learned behavior of screaming, hollering, losing their temper, bullying, having their own way, and fighting everybody is not to be tolerated.

621. God is challenging us to be our very, very best. Living on the earth is a test, and God is expecting us to pass every test of character. He's preparing us to be with Him throughout eternity.

622. When people come to your home, be hospitable, and help them to relax by offering them water or tea or soda.

623. The true end of life and the true scope of life is God. It must start with God and end with God.

624. All of this is about food. God wants you to know that according to Scripture, Genesis 9:3, Romans 14:14, and Mark 7:19–21 all confirm that it is okay to eat whatever you want; just pray over it and sanctify it with the Word of God. Sometimes, of course, your doctor may have to limit your habits on eating certain foods because they may not be good for you.

625. The three most important words in any relationship are "I was wrong."

626. It's going to be impossible to be in any relationship without offending people. You will not be perfect.

627. If a person has been wounded, if a family has been wounded, if a complete nation or people has been wounded, then the wound is still open and needs to be attended to and healed. Reparations are needed, and healing must be administered too before the wound is healed. This may take years, but ignoring the offense will not make the wound go away, America.

628. When apologies have been genuinely offered, then some assurances and adjustments will be given. When people mess up royally in a relationship, especially a marriage relationship, they want to be forgiven instantly. However, you must realize that hurt and pain are still alive. People need time to heal; therefore, you will have to wait until the healing process is over, and you

will have to make sure you understand that you have to pay the price to rebuild trust again. Relationships will not be the same, but the good news is that they can be extremely better.

629. God's assignments for us are in progressive stages.

630. Needless to say, to be blessed, it is evident that some persecution comes with it.

631. Much prayer is needed in everything you do in life; I repeat, much prayer is needed in everything you do in this life.

632. God is the only true provider of love, joy, peace, and everlasting life.

633. You can be educated but not godly wise, moral, and intelligent.

634. Fifty-nine men were founders of the Declaration of Independence, and twenty-nine of them had seminary degrees.

635. To be intelligent, you must have good judgment and sound thought. Work on having a brilliant mind.

636. The Scripture says in Isaiah 19:25 (KJV), "Whom the LORD of hosts shall bless, saying, Blessed be Egypt my people, and Assyria the work of my hands, and Israel mine inheritance."

637. Meekness is not being weak at all. Meekness is humility, maturity, self-control, wisdom, strength, and discipline.

638. Always ask the Lord to correct you in justice and not with anger.

639. Men are to be conquerors, leaders, and providers.

640. Be like Solomon; ask the Lord to fill you with the spirit of wisdom.

641. The Urim and the Thummim were sacred lots that gave a yes or no answer from God (Exodus 28:30).

642. It is good to think highly of yourself but do not think more highly than you ought.

643. One of the highest callings there is, is to be sent from a local church to do work for God.

644. The very foundation, the very beginning of wisdom, is to honor and revere God. God's Word says that out of the mouth of God comes wisdom, knowledge, and understanding. If we don't have the wisdom, knowledge, and understanding of God, how can we properly and adequately serve or be a complete blessing to humanity, especially to our families? God's wisdom will surprisingly turn out to be a great help to our nerves and will moisture our bones (Proverbs 3:8).

645. It is said that a wicked person that is full of rebellion can't go to sleep unless they have done something wrong. Your own wickedness will punish you, and your own backsliding ways will rebuke you. True repentance means to change your mind, think differently, regret your sin, and change your conduct.

646. The six things that the Lord hates (there are indeed seven of them) are: an abomination to Him or detestable to Him, are a proud look, a lying tongue, hands that shed innocent blood, a heart that divisive or manufactured wicked thoughts and plans, feet that are swift to run to mischief and evil, a false witness that speaks lies and he that soweth discord among the brethren.

647. Believe me, everything that feels good initially will not prove to be good for you. Wake up!

648. You can transcend your limitations.

649. Never tell yourself you can't do a certain thing. In fact, let other people be the ones who say, "Who does she think she is; she can't do that." You can do all things through Christ, who strengthens you.

650. Ask the Lord in prayer to heal all 200 billion neurons in your brain. Ask Him to touch and heal every transmitter and every receptor in Jesus' name. This will start the healing of traumatic damage that's been done in your life. Receive the power of God.

651. Have an overcoming mentality.

652. Enjoy and celebrate small accomplishments as well as big accomplishments. Being in your promised land will necessitate seeing giants, and you must not back away from spiritual battles because wealth is in your promised land.

653. Don't spend time on things you don't have control over. Focus not on the things that you can't affect but focus on the things that you can affect.

654. For business owners, it will be wise for you to designate an account for people that work for you to have training in human relations. This could possibly double your productivity.

655. When a person is not serving or working, life is meaningless; but when they are serving and working, life begins to be fulfilled.

656. To maximize your personal and professional effectiveness, you must develop the right habits.

657. Needless to say, the church is still a noble occupation, and it should be an exciting place to be a part of. It is a place to reflect right values, focus on the giving of ourselves, and it's part of our calling.

658. Walking in love produces a clean life.

659. In an insecure, confused, and deceived world, a person that has the right standards is a light and a stabilizing force.

660. Make a life for yourself and not just a living. Work should not be the only thing that defines you.

661. People that ultimately accomplish many things in life are those that stick to it, no matter what.

662. Spontaneity also helps you take advantage of opportunities. It brings richness into your life.

663. The traits of jealousy can be destructive to your personality.

664. Don't be completely moved by what you see or hear; only be moved by what you believe.

665. Daughters will always need their fathers to provide wisdom and advice.

666. Pride keeps a person from worshiping God. We are used to being our own God.

667. With wisdom, knowledge, and understanding, we don't have to run from any problems any longer.

668. Without a doubt, when you do things that are wrong, you allow the devil to use you.

669. Laws of God are called principles.

670. People can be your example, but be yourself.

671. Forgiveness is not just something you do; it has to become a mindset, a lifestyle.

672. Waiting also means to continue to serve.

673. The joy that comes from heaven will never be dictated by circumstances.

674. Whenever the Jewish celebrations happen, and you may see Jews blowing the shofar horn, Satan thinks it is the last trumpet, and Jesus is returning. It makes him very nervous. Deep inside, he also knows his time is at hand, and the lake of fire is his guaranteed destiny.

675. If you dwell on people's shortcomings, this will destroy you. This mindset must change, and you must focus on *people's potential* and the wonderful things that they do; that's good.

676. Men, don't play with women's emotions; don't tell them that you love them, that you're going to marry them, or that you're going to do anything if you're not going to do it. Don't insinuate promises. Don't lead them on, and don't play with their emotions!

677. I am also here to remind you that Jesus experienced every pain, and He overcame it, and because He is in your life, you can overcome any pain as well.

678. Divide and conquer has always been the end of the enemy's number one strategy. Don't let him divide and keep you away from God and His church.

679. Seek God's love and kindness because it is better than life.

680. Ladies, be kind to each other. I have seen how women tend to treat each other, and it simply hurts as a man to see it, knowing how emotional, gentle and sensitive you are. This is not all women, but I have seen enough. Please be more cordial, loving, accepting, etc. To the brothers, the same goes. We have to stop hurting each other. What I see is simply self-hatred. Yes, there are so many variables involved in the root cause, but if we just choose love, respect, and not be so hostile towards each other, one brother at a time. We can change all of this.

681. Quick-tempered people commit foolish acts. People that are always angry have a distorted view of life. Their perspective is completely erroneous. You must start seeing things as God sees them.

682. If you are continually failing in a certain area in life, it means that you do not have the proper knowledge concerning whatever it is. It is as simple as that. Start over and get the true facts. If the chips fall on your attitude, it's time to do something about it. *Change!*

683. If you are still holding grudges from childhood, this means that you think that every family member is perfect and all parents are perfect. This is not the case.

684. Don't provoke and support anger; provoke love, peace, and friendship.

685. A soft answer turns away wrath, but grievous words stir up anger. Soft answers will stop the devil in his tracts; try it. A

woman told me once that when her husband wanted to argue. She said she would tell him, "Go ahead and argue, and when you get to when I am to respond, you just go right ahead and say my part because I'm going to bed." I thought that was classic. By the way, I asked Karen if I could use this.

686. Salvation is not complete until you receive the baptism of the Holy Spirit and become a disciple/taught child of God. Tell your pastor you want to learn all there is to learn about the Bible.

687. Everyone responds to love.

688. A wise man will deal with his own conscience.

689. When we practice forgiving, forgiving becomes easier.

690. A joyous family is only brought about by the continual use of biblical principles. There are many social and religious organizations that highlight ethics and morals but refuse to connect the God of the Bible or Jesus. This is still futile. You need the Living God on your side and in your life. They build these cults using the universe as the ultimate source. So, when the highly suggested character and moral principles are used, and they see they experience the benefits, the leaders claim this as the total validity and confirmations of their idol gods.

691. Many times, you want your teenager to sit down and give many paragraphs in communication, but most teenagers will give one-word answers, and that's it. They are mostly okay.

692. Having your children be part of groups, clubs, and teams in the schools helps them tremendously. Encourage this with your children.

693. Introverted people mainly don't tell folks when they have been hurt. This must stop. That is a weakness that must be eradicated and corrected.

694. Accept people that you love always, put up with their imperfections, never stop loving them and never stop praying for them. People have put up with us with all of our shortcomings as we continue to become better people.

695. If you have problems with anger and are quick-tempered, ask God to help you. You have to realize that you live in a world of imperfect people. Believe it or not, you are one of 7 billion.

696. Just because you've been hurt several times in relationships, don't let this stop you and keep you holding back on love and being loved. Stay vulnerable. Loving relationships are worth it. When you are hurt, ask the Lord to heal your heart and erase the pain. He will, and time will help also. It's called *life*.

697. The Word of God is so alive that it became a human being, Jesus.

698. It is erroneous to only seek fulfillment, things, and accumulation. We then miss the purpose and meaning of life. Watch it; materialism is eating the western world alive. Building a life around complete pleasure is simply not going to satisfy you in the long run.

699. Responsible leadership positions carry substantial criticism, both fair and unfair. This is why I love and I have great respect for godly and moral leaders.

700. Allow senior subordinates to unburden themselves around you.

701. Build your definition of success on true values. If there are true values, believe me, there are also false values.

702. Standing up for true principles help make you a person of true pleasure, true power, true prestige, true prosperity, and true position.

703. Great cultures fall because prosperity leads the people into apathy, laziness, and ingratitude. Eventually, this permeates the values and ethics, and entire cultures collapse. Erosion of moral values is devastating.

704. Our culture and city are looking for true leadership, people of vision, moral courage, values, ethics, fairness, godliness, and righteousness.

705. Society reflects the health of major institutions, which reflect the health of our families, which reflect the moral health of individuals.

706. Compliments of affirming words, not flattery; please, release at least one a day.

707. Don't live a life on fickle choices of chance.

708. Discipline is needed to help people have self-control. You must teach the difference between right and wrong.

709. The emotional foundation of love is trust.

710. One of the most important sources of happiness in your life will be the one you allow to be close to your heart. Savor the time you spend together.

711. When you connect with faith, life becomes much more vivid. You begin to see things for what they really are. You quickly find that you aren't as perfect as you thought.

712. Are you lonely, or are you alone? When you are alone, you have the time to enhance your uniqueness and pursue your destiny unhindered. Treasure your alone time and identify it correctly.

713. Remember, the only thing that should validate your worth is that God, the almighty God had a say in creating you. Money, fame, things, and power can't touch your divine validation and standard of value. Know this every day you wake up.

714. To be loved by others, do for them what you'd want them to do for you. This will identify you as a source of pleasure, and everyone loves those who bring them pleasure!

715. Show people that you appreciate them by saying phrases like "I'm glad you came" and "I love the things you say." They are very interesting and encouraging.

716. The most effective way to be loved is to master giving encouragement and making people feel special. Give what others fail to give and say things that others fail to say.

717. Two of the greatest gifts you can give someone are wisdom and knowledge.

718. True love and fellowship brings unity, and unity brings power and the blessing of God.

719. Young people, if you want more wisdom, pay close attention to all your teachers. Refuse to be distracted.

720. Being righteous reveal and unveils the path that leads you to divine open doors and success.

721. Be kind because everybody is fighting the battle of life. Kindness is very refreshing.

722. "Faithful" refers to unchangeableness and denotes firmness or constancy. It is being committed to keeping your promises; therefore, you become worthy of people's trust.

723. Faith is also firm belief, assurance, persuasion, trust, conviction, and confidence in God.

724. Being loved means feeling connected, respected, valued, and a sense of belonging. Cared for! When a person doesn't experience love, studies show that your biological systems get overwhelmed. Social isolation leads to higher depression.

725. The greatest benefit of love is joy! It's a fact that happiness depends more on the quality of family relationships *than on the level of income.*

726. The world is obsessed with sports, entertainment, gossip, trivial diversion, and faceless media but is more isolated

than ever before. With all of our flashy tech-savviness, great denominations, and all we have accomplished, we have become colder and impersonal.

727. Don't worry about what you can't understand; some things were not meant for you to understand.

728. Bless your children with a special prayer for economic creativity and spiritual steadfastness.

729. Everything that comes to your mind is not completely true. Everything you feel does not necessarily mean what you are feeling. For example, I don't feel important, or I don't feel people love me. The truth many times are far from what you feel.

730. Your responses to offenses will show the level of your maturity.

731. No matter what happens, God will only operate in love. The true test is, will you respond like God?

732. People are the church, but the buildings are holy dwelling places of God.

733. Believe means to accept something as true, presume, assume, be convinced by, trust, have confidence in, adhere to, trust in, rely on, consider honest, and give credence to. (You can also mental assent, meaning to believe that some things simply exist and have no confidence and trust at all in them. Many people are like Satan; they believe there is a God but will not adhere to His guidance.)

734. God commands us; keep all your spiritual doors shut, so the enemy can't intrude into your life. Dare to say and do the right things, especially when you are being tried.

735. Your city's problems must become your problem, so do what it takes to help resolve them. You and I will ultimately and eternally be identified with our generation and our nation. What did we do to make a change?

736. The ultimate call on your life is to become righteous.

737. The greatest need of any teenager is wisdom. With the various pitfalls and challenges every teenager faces in today's world, teenagers need all the wisdom they can get. Wisdom not only shows the teenager or young adult how to avoid failure and heartache but also how to achieve success and satisfaction in life. The greatest source of wisdom for teenagers is the Book of Proverbs. In fact, the Book of Proverbs is the only book of the Bible written specifically for teenagers. It is the original self-help and character-building book for teenagers. In the Book of Proverbs, we also find a wealth of practical knowledge.

738. The lips of the righteous feed many, but fools die for lack of sense.

739. Wisdom, *activated wisdom*, **produces** *"ability,"* the ability to judge correctly and to follow the best course of action based on knowledge and understanding. True heaven-sent wisdom is the ability to see something from God's viewpoint. Wisdom is "God's character." Wisdom is the knowledge and the ability to make the right choices at the opportune time. By the way, the *consistency* of making the right choice is an indication of one's spiritual maturity. *Wise people* are not sluggards, fools, or simpletons. A wise man can also be identified as the way he handles or operates concerning money.

740. When one discovers the outpouring of the wisdom of God, confusion, deception, and ignorance immediately dispels, and he finds life and lives more abundantly.

741. One that seeks to get unrighteous money will bring destruction to his home.

742. Wisdom declares that money can't buy true friends; the so-called friends will forsake you in trouble or when your money is gone.

743. Your greatest battles in life are designed to get you away from wisdom.

744. Your destiny truly includes abundance if you are not deceived.

745. Eagles don't hang out with chickens.

746. People in authority are supposed to be those who perfect, encourage, challenge, motivate, and coach people to be all that they can be.

747. Before you follow the wisdom of others, ask the question, where did you get your wisdom? Who told you the things that you passionately operate by?

748. The coldest winters bring the greatest springs.

749. Beware, this world's lower wisdom will call the godly wise out of touch, narrow-minded, nonintellectual, escapist, and judgmental. It will happen.

750. Most people ask for more out of a relationship than they can give.

751. Become a smart person, living a life of beneficial deeds.

752. Correction improves the quality of life for everyone. Be part of organizations that will correct you.

753. The more wisdom you know and do, the more fulfilled you will become.

754. In everyone's life is a divine deposit of greatness waiting to be recognized, discovered, and multiplied.

755. . You must review individual wisdoms until they are internalized and not placed on a shelf. It will begin to become the way you live and help confirm your greatness.

756. Wrong conduct will have you doing what you never thought you would do, staying longer than you want and going farther than you want to go.

757. Work like you are already debt-free, love like you have an unlimited resource, and dance like you are free as a bird.

758. If we don't love, we become self-centered and demanding.

759. Why should we pray when God knows all things? So we can activate our Covenant.

760. In arguments, stay until you find solutions and enhance the strength of the union. Take time-outs when it gets too heated and when it seems fights may occur. What is most particularly destructive is the sneering, body motions, eye-rolling, and correcting grammar instead of dealing with the nature of the argument. Staying and not running says you are committed to finding a solution. Staying shows that you want to strengthen the relationship.

761. Do not judge anyone until you have been in their shoes.

762. Help people feel you really value them. Watch how you look at people. You, therefore, reassure them and put them at ease. It helps us connect with others; this is a civic duty. I emphasize this because some people have a mean countenance sometimes.

763. Couples, save the big discussions for when you are relaxed, not hungry, stressed, and tired. Don't talk about problems or bills as soon as your spouse gets home. Let them unwind first.

764. Try looking deeper into people, for nothing is what it appears to be.

765. When highly tensed and stressed out, you need to laugh; it causes a major release of tension, gloom, aggravation, depression, and worry. Use it to break tension on others and cause them to focus on anything better. Laughter rescues us from bad experiences. Laughter loosens us up and helps us forget our anxieties, and breaks down stubborn walls. Make sure you watch at least a few comedy shows each week.

766. Never make fun of anyone. You hurt their soul. Be careful. Some people can't handle that at all.

767. Many people in this society are worried about Russia, China, Iran, North Korea, crooked politicians, nuclear war, economy, time bombs, downsizing, taxes, ISIS, etc. One prominent leader in our society was asked the question, "If you could start over, what would you do?" His immediate answer was, "I would not worry as much as I have." He said that most of the bad things he feared never happened; they never did.

768. Our greatest commodity is time. We must stop wasting so much of it. One main area where we absorb crazy hours of time is on the internet and playing games. We have to get a handle on this. Read a book, indulge in live conversations, or look into starting a side business. You have the time to do it. Just stop wasting so much of it.

769. Just helping others make us better human beings.

770. Remember, when people are doing badly, they are literally hurting themselves the most.

771. When you enlighten people, it changes their perspective, and their actions follow.

772. Being interested in others develops trust and makes them open up to you. Just the fact you care develops admiration.

773. When you are honest, you will not lose the opportunity to be intimate with people.

774. People that love you want two things to happen; they want you to become wise and wealthy.

775. When you are wise, people will be fascinated with every word that comes from your mouth. Life will become more pleasant, lively, and valuable.

776. Wisdom is the yeast of survival. Every drop of it enhances your life.

777. Learn from all people.

778. Wise people are not pseudo-philosophers or para-philosophers. Wise people deal mainly with the purpose of life, humanity, and potential for greatness.

779. Be cautious with people you entrust your emotional and spiritual health.

780. Be bothered by the effects of ignorance and unwise thought; go looking for wisdom.

781. The greatest of all discoveries is the availability of God's wisdom. You will not get godly wisdom from anyone that doesn't have a relationship with the God of the Bible. That's a fact. Don't waste your time asking them anything about godly wisdom.

782. Do what you love, and it will guide you to your purpose.

783. Integrity from you will draw honesty from others.

784. Continue to nurture yourself; this will bring insurance and protect the fizzle.

785. Deep relationships share dreams, fears, expectations, and happiness.

786. Without trust, relationships weaken and dissolve.

787. What you cry about in society is normally a key to what you are here to solve.

788. Never be completely satisfied with less than best. You are worth it. However, as you progress, stay in line with a budget and what you can afford. Avoid foolish spending. Never give anyone your credit card.

789. Use credit cards, however, to support you whenever they are needed. Pay off the balance each month. This is the appropriate way to use a credit card. Extravagant use is abuse and will destroy your credit and place you in financial prison for years.

790. When visiting your spouse's family, make sure you are friendly and encouraging. *If you don't talk*, you will be considered unfriendly and too proud to indulge. Be complementary and ask questions about their accomplishments and their interest. *Never* tell your spouse it's time to leave. You are with them all the time. Let them enjoy their time with their family. This also goes for when they are with their friends. It's extremely embarrassing and selfish when you jump up and want your spouse to leave before they want to.

791. Let your spouse have friends and let your friends have other friends. Quit trying to dominate other people's lives. This is called "mind control."

792. Life is so much happier when we choose to forget horrible past experiences.

793. Horror movies produce strange and very uncomfortable experiences for you and your children.

794. Just because people are old, it doesn't mean they are smart or wise. Sorry.

795. Allow your spouse to pursue every endeavor they desire. Just make sure it doesn't destroy your financial future. You don't want to get into your senior years, and they blame you for not allowing them to complete their dreams. You want them to brag about how you supported them completely.

796. My suggestion for couples who could not have children on their own is to adopt at least one child. You don't want to get older and have no one to pour your support, life, and wisdom into.

797. A house is a structure, but a home is a place where love is to be preserved, commitment is exemplified, and respect is treasured. Build and preserve a home.

798. You will never have in your life what you are not willing to work for. Therefore, quit blaming others for your own laziness. You might have to start over. That's okay.

799. Make yourself exciting, fun, and pleasant to be around. Quit being like a boring knot on a log. That's your job to make this change. This is why you have this book in your hands. Use these principles. Start here. Read and apply all the principles of wisdom in this book.

800. People say, "This is just who I am," just to keep from changing and refining themselves. Your lifelong job is to produce the best you possible. Your weaknesses should be the first things to deal with and improve.

801. Quit using designer clothes, fine cars, money, and identifying yourself with groups, etc., to replace epic character building. Enhance yourself!

802. Learn (how) to say *no* when you know you don't have time to satisfy everyone's request. Just tell them how much is on your plate, and you just don't have the time. You can also tell people you are busy and not reveal that you are busy getting needed rest.

803. When you are angry with someone, it is never right to destroy their property, burn their car or puncture their tires. This is wild and wrong. When relationships are toxic and you seem to butt heads often, it simply means you were not predestined to be together.

804. Are you a person that uses your family's accomplishments to identify as yours? Develop your own. It is never too late to begin. People will help you if you show a serious commitment to growing up and being an adult. Many live a bratty, spoiled life. Let's change that before it's too late.

805. *Slick* people really think others don't see their dishonest ways. Everyone sees them. Just because they may not say anything does not mean they don't see your deception.

806. There are many smart, wise, and moral people that may not have a college education. They may not be able to articulate like you, but they are very wise and intelligent.

807. As long as you can afford it, take well-calculated risks. You don't want to get in your senior years and regret it.

808. Values are there to support you and keep you safe when times are rough and when you get to be *wealthy*.

809. It's okay with God to marry outside of your race. You will have to keep in mind there will be some additional challenges you may have to deal with. Also, be ready to get used to and enjoy a different culture. It was forbidden once because God wanted Jesus to come through the lineage of the Jewish people by the flesh. His natural and spiritual father was God the Father.

810. Absolutely nothing can take the place of persistence.

811. If you completely fail and blow it, start over, own up to your error, learn from it and get back into the game of life. Don't get in a rut of despair and stay there. Get up and get back in the game! You will feel bad, but that horrible feeling will subside as time goes on. Everyone has messed up royally, sometimes.

812. Dating is for eventually getting married. It has a strategic purpose. Dating is not to be perpetual and aimless. When you shack, however, you disrespect that women's family. If they are good enough to shack with, they are good enough to marry.

813. Compassion is also sympathizing and caring with people that are struggling and hurting badly. It involves sacrificing valuable time; face it. People with great insecurities falsely think that being compassionate is a weakness.

814. Dads and moms are to teach their children excellence. Whatever you do is worth doing it right the first time or not at all.

815. Key values are: integrity, commitment, loyalty, and responsibility.

816. A half-truth has always been a whole lie.

817. You are to never make money or advance your interest at (any) cost. Never sell your soul for money, fame, or prestige.

818. Having too many friends will question and put a strain on your integrity. You won't have the time to adequately support the needs.

819. Words are not designed or multiplied to be used without wisdom.

820. Hearing is receiving and perceiving sound, but listening requires consideration. Your brain is to be processing meaning from the words that are being said. You consciously choose to listen with the intention of understanding. This is called the "art of communication."

821. Studied people want brilliant information based on researched absolutes.

822. We must have strong and honorable character always while doing what we are supposed to do. You will be challenged quite often to get off track by being unethical. Don't ever do it. The real you is the person that is tempted when no one is watching. Also, when you do things illegal or unethical with other people, they can hang this over your head for the rest of your life. Young people, never take nude pictures with anyone.

823. Characteristic traits include endurance, justice, bearing, tact, initiative, coolness, improvement, drive, confidence, decisiveness, and courage.

824. Even God is longsuffering, but not *forever* suffering.

825. There is no end to the good you can do. There is enough love in you to love all the people in the entire world. However, it does not mean you are to burn yourself out completely while trying to satisfy everyone.

826. Global conditions require proper leadership. Every dire condition of humanity is a result of poor leadership.

827. Fifty-five percent of the families in America are dysfunctional in something but are held responsible for producing functional communities and citizens. As a result of poor leadership, many have developed destructive attitudes and perspectives that dominate their lives.

828. Many of our precious people are angry because of their inability to deal appropriately with their lives. They just don't know the "how-tos" in life.

829. When you begin to believe the best in others, offense tends to leave.

830. Much of what you see in the inner city is the result of inadequate security, support, and much depravation.

831. You can't possibly continue to hate someone you are praying for.

832. The way to a women's heart is through properly understanding her emotions.

833. Every conflict can be seen as a test. Perspective is everything.

834. The Lord loves us too much to be carrying on like we sometimes do.

835. Work is valuable beyond its money-generating benefits. It keeps you vitally involved in life and part of the community of helping others, all of which are necessary for survival and longevity.

836. To succeed in business means you need to know how the world works. The Bible is a comprehensive guide on how the world works. Make sure you learn all there is about the profession as well. Many people get too spiritual and won't do their due diligence as far as learning the business principles that produce successful businesses. You need to do more than have faith and prayer. Use these wisdoms. Ultimately, all wisdoms come from above.

837. Only be influenced by values, truth, and professional opinions.

838. People become judgmental, unloving, emotionally distant, condemning, and rejecting because of abnormal child-rearing.

839. The daily needs of a child are affirmation, security, affection, praise, encouragement, support, love, and quality time. Never give up on your child.

840. Affirmations also include a hug, acceptance, an arm around the shoulder, gentle roughhousing, or wrestling on the living room floor.

841. Most mistakes can be healed through repentance and apologies.

842. Signs of good mental health include being able to function well intellectually, emotionally, physically, and spiritually. Also, carefully consider the mental health of an individual before you get married to them.

843. Healing also includes an exceptional response to individual responsibility and the acknowledgment of the best individual choices.

844. The following contribute to stress: job issues, marital problems, school issues, and financial problems.

845. One form of abuse breeds another.

846. If wrong attitudes are not corrected, they will escalate; eventually destroying the perpetrator and everyone they associate with.

847. It is your active responsibility to make sure your house and property appreciate in value.

848. Stocks are more volatile than bonds.

849. Anger in a meeting shows a lack of intelligence.

850. When talking with people in business, look them straight in the eye, confirm contracts, and demand (time-oriented guarantees) and agreements. Nothing is legally binding unless it's written and signed. Tell them you are looking forward to them being people of excellence.

851. Most attorneys will negotiate their fees.

852. Ask for references when dealing with contractors.

853. Tools that build a nation are love, compassion, holiness, goodness, unity, and justice.

854. Supreme principles came from a supreme place called heaven.

855. Corrupt character has caused more pain than all the national disasters put together.

856. When you know you are loved, it should bring emotional overflow and relaxation. God loves you, and nothing you can ever do will stop Him from loving you. He may not approve of our conduct, but He loves you because He is love. That's what He does. In this life, you will need supernatural strength, and God will provide it for His children. His commandments are to become our amazing counselors.

857. Where there is no vision, people perish.

858. If the church you attend does not satisfy your spiritual hunger and thirst, ask the Lord to lead you to the right one. The 200-year-old family church just may not be the one.

859. You must understand the times and what you are to do in this society.

860. Obey them that have rule over you. The Bible says in Hebrews 13:17 (KJV), "Obey them [pastors] that have the rule over you, and submit yourselves: for they watch for your souls, as they that must give account, that they may do it with joy, and not with grief: for that is unprofitable for you."

861. Your self-worth is not the sum total of your mistakes, misfortunes, and failures. It's all of what God says you are. This is only found in the holy Scriptures.

862. Low-quality work is also a sign of low self-esteem.

863. When providing couple counseling, make sure you ideally have both parties present. Be balanced and keep from completely judging the entire matter until both parties are available.

864. Prayer is a conversation, even a speech unto the profoundly impressive God. He is also the perfection of beauty.

865. As we ask daily for forgiveness, it also means that we must render forgiveness.

866. Never compare yourself with other people. Be the best you. Nobody can build the best you. This is what the world needed when God made you. Then you will be very comfortable and satisfied being you.

867. Where there is sin and iniquities, you will also find sickness and disease. Yes, sin and iniquity produce sickness and disease too.

868. The most intimate thing two people can do is pray. If you want to know the true heart of a person, listen to their prayers.

869. Five types of fools: one that doesn't believe in God, a rebel, a scoffer, an arrogant, and one that devotes their life to folly.

870. Euthanasia, mercy killing, is wrong.

871. When spiritual pollution is in your home, there are nightmares, constant arguments, restless children, unexplained illnesses, ghosts, and foul odors. Know that horror movies, reading Harry Potter books, séances, and witchcraft can contribute to this. A spiritual house cleaning is needed. Seek your local church.

872. A man that lacks understanding and is held in honor is like a beast that perishes.

873. The more we abstain from wrong, the more honor is bestowed upon our lives.

874. Honor is also in the form of a check, vacations, when we are invited to see someone's home, greeted with a smile, given flowers, a handshake with a smile, or when hugs are given to us. Don't overlook this. Then, show genuine gratitude.

875. Remember, it is always too soon to quit. When all else fails, begin again. Give up every idea of quitting. Champions force themselves to do what they might not want to do in the heat of competition. Many of life's failures are individuals who did not realize how close they were to success when they gave up.

876. Becoming self-sufficient is more about choices and not chance.

877. King David gave an equivalent of 100 million dollars in one offering for the building of God's temple. Not bad for someone who started off with five stones and a slingshot, right?

878. When we choose a lifestyle of being wrong, a spirit of displeasure will be upon us.

879. If kings needed prophets to make major decisions in running their kingdoms back in their day, we surely need them today in running our lives. A pastor is a type of prophet. Therefore, as we keep our eyes on God's advice, we will always walk on water, meaning we will see the supernatural manifest in our lives.

880. When we walk in unity, we make the impossible possible.

881. God is too wise to make mistakes and too loving to be unkind.

882. Roots of bitterness only defile you. Release unforgiveness and offense. Let it go!

883. If your business is not a moral, noble, or worthy work, it will taunt your entire existence. When you feel good about your profession, your enthusiasm will sweep others into what you are doing. If you are embarrassed about your business, you set yourself up to fail.

884. True wealth follows large-scale righteous conduct.

885. Instill yourself with serving others; it brings a joy that can compare with giving a gift.

886. You need a position that you can be passionate about. You can also engage in ongoing community-building projects.

887. Maximize your interaction with others. It's a camouflage for building relationships.

888. Don't be overly focused on your hourly wage but on your employer. Help him sell his business.

889. We must return to seeing businesses and businessmen as being heroic and not camp on their negative views.

890. There is a hunger in America for community and relationships.

891. Be always punctual. If you can't, always extend the courtesy of calling if you will be late. Don't take the attitude "five minutes won't hurt; they will wait." You can blow a billion-dollar deal because you were thirty seconds late.

892. Remember this: sometimes things you really need may be inside of someone you don't enjoy.

893. Evil's greatest fear is righteousness and true genuine relationship.

894. If you change what you know, you will change what you do.

895. Serious businesses build websites; eBay gross billions each year.

896. Who is it that one who darkens counsel without divine knowledge?

897. Most people don't get in trouble building what they need. They get in trouble getting too many things they want or feel they deserve.

898. We live in a society whereby people are safe and comfortable around those that are stepping up, moving forward, and not stagnating. People that simply make things happen instead of criticizing and talking about those that do.

899. Emotional needs are needs that, when they are skillfully administered, make people feel amazing.

900. Thoughts of a wicked person are abominations.

901. We are not required to be successful, but we are required to try.

902. Most fear old age, but it is said that most major accomplishments happen in your old age.

903. The things you will remember most will come from the context of love acts towards someone else or love acts from others to you.

904. The key motivation for all we do must be Agape love.

905. Wealth is a great servant but a terrible master.

906. Our culture should never omit the awesome and wonderful God of the Bible. Many want to eliminate everything about God because they want to stay in their dark and unhealthy sin. God owns it all and must be placed back into it all. That is our job to make it restore.

907. Unfortunately, the development of natural science has also undermined the belief in the spiritual and miraculous. They have brought into question the authority of all sacred writings. The crown of creation was to help God in perfecting His world. This is why He gifted us with intellectual and moral freedoms.

908. God says welcoming a stranger is better than welcoming His glory. This is how much He loves people.

909. Have the courage to be different from others. Sometimes you will be the only one to do what's right.

910. Sex without commitment is considered unworthy for human beings.

911. When a person refuses transformation, change, and progression, then they are stuck, and they choose to have a mediocre, mundane, and whatever kind of life.

912. Appreciate every moment of life; it doesn't matter if things are not going the way you want.

913. Let laziness and apathy make you want to run.

914. If you don't take control of your own life, common situations, people, and circumstances will. You will be moved by every wind and storm.

915. Many people erroneously feel that there is nothing else to learn after college. That's a shame.

916. Many prefer to be comfortable and unhappy rather than endure the discomfort of changing a habit.

917. What you believe is what you will say; therefore, what you say will come from the past. This is why we must change our belief system to experience the better things in life.

918. A man's word is his bond; integrity must become his lifestyle.

919. Transparency will help all of your relationships soar.

920. Never desire or accept a position without accepting and mastering the responsibilities.

921. Never speak against your leadership.

922. Meditate on success principles, meaning memorize, mutter, and think on them.

923. If you have not been to any organized learning center to learn *how* to be a father, mother, great friend, husband, wife, etc., how do you think your relationship will ever have a chance of prospering? We need to learn about the many success principles of relationships, just like we do with our professions.

924. People thrive when they are truly connected with what they love doing.

925. One way to judge prophecy is, does it glorify Jesus? Realize that even though a prophecy comes to pass, it does not mean it came from God. All miraculous events do not come from God. Other strong spirits exist that can mimic and produce spiritual manifestations. You must be able to make correct discernment. The church will teach you this.

926. People are easily deceived because they desire recognition, soulish gain, and a position without responsibility.

927. Ouija boards pose as a game, but in reality, it is a forbidden occult practice.

928. Always correct in gentle Agape love.

929. Obedience is a form of safety and protection.

930. A home divided cannot stand.

931. Anyone who accepts a duty, large or small, must be completely faithful and perform it very well. If you are responsible for cleaning, then be the best the world has ever seen.

932. Responsibility is the source of having rights.

933. Pioneers experience agonizing loneliness. Very few have the convictions; therefore, pioneers walk alone.

934. Injustice anywhere is a threat to injustice everywhere.

935. Digging into the principles of faith softens the heart.

936. People are desperate for kindness, service, and connection.

937. Judge not according to appearance.

938. Ultimate character also includes longsuffering. It's waiting for the best to be manifested.

939. Each day, make living a successful life a priority. Determination, discipline, and perseverance are needed to accomplish this.

940. No commitment, no success.

941. Stay focused and endure everything that comes your way. If it came to you, it means you can not only handle it, and you can completely soar above it.

942. Emotionally injured people must also be goal-oriented and risk-takers to be involved in healing themselves.

943. Never degrade tough masculine behavior. Let men be men.

944. Jesus was nice, assertive, tough, courageous, and protective. Mimic Him.

945. Change is the greatest element of character.

946. People respect those that take a stand.

947. An always defensive strategy does not produce ultimate victory. We must be offensive and preventive.

948. What is important is not luxury but love, not wealth but wisdom, not gold but goodness.

949. Abomination is what is utterly despised. Let's not be part of anything despised. It will cause your heart and consciousness to become seared. This is dangerous.

950. Fathers need to be involved in the moral discipline, teaching, and moral guidance of their children.

951. Quality time has been proven to be more effective than the quantity of time.

952. We, as men, have the responsibility of portraying God to our children. It's a fact a child sees God exactly how they see their father.

953. Rid yourself of an innumerable amount of unproven theories. We are simply tired of them and tired of being duped and lied to.

954. Worship services should be the greatest celebrated weekly event in every country. Every member should be taking part in it.

955. Our cities need people of moral courage and values.

956. The Bible reminds us in Hebrews 6:10 (GNT), "God is not unfair. He will not forget the work you did or the love you showed for him in the help you gave and are still giving to other Christians."

957. Socialism is one step away from complete government takeover.

958. "Redeemed" means bought back, rescued, recovered, vindicated, and reclaimed.

959. Freedom of speech does not mean we are to neglect morals and ethics when we speak.

960. You have a right to never have to fear anything or anybody.

961. Peace is a *who* and not an event. God is to be your peace. It can always be maintained in all situations and circumstances.

962. The possession of wisdom is far above rubies or pearls.

963. Socialism will make the government your God.

964. Don't ever be one to use dark principles. You will pay much more than you were granted.

965. Departing from evil is a sign of understanding.

966. When you are in bad relationships with your parents, your mind and outcomes in life will be greatly distressed and hindered. Heal this relationship quickly. Sometimes you might have to initiate reconciliation, and you weren't wrong. Do it anyway. You need this relationship healed for your total success with God. If they were totally wrong, give it to God. Many will not apologize either. But don't worry about it. Let it go. Ask the Lord to heal your heart, and He will.

967. The path of the wrongdoer: they can prosper, but a curse is upon their prosperity; even if their children receive it, it will diminish.

968. When you make God wrong and yourself right, you make yourself better than God. Watch it!

969. Many limit the possession of wisdom to themselves.

970. When you open your mouth and fill it with God's Word, you bring life, stability, light, hope, happiness, and wisdom to the ears of all who listen to you.

971. The deep wisdom of the Bible brings ethics, morals, and timeless values into your life. This is called living higher.

972. People need your mercy and grace.

973. Good parenting does not mean giving your children a perfect life. It means teaching them to lead a good and happy life in an

imperfect world. When they come to you with a problem, stop and listen to them.

974. Short cuddles with your children last forever.

975. Serve and give to God, through the church, (only) because you love Him. He desires genuine love. However, God says in Proverbs 8:21 (KJV), "That I may cause those that love me to inherit substance; and I will fill their treasures."

976. Many say that life comes from random chance and fate, but the wise knows differently.

977. Flattery is designed to entice and manipulate.

978. Encouragement sustains the weary. It sees gifts and strengths and affirms them in specific terms.

979. It is not the many words we are to use to bless people but the weight of the ones used.

980. Unity is born of shared commitments and values that are foundational and convictional.

981. Through faith and patience, one must wait for great things to manifest and come to fruition.

982. Each day, as we love others, we live out our friendship with God.

983. When repentance and restoration happen, an abundance of joy is restored.

984. When God is in question, remember He is never surprised at what happens on the earth. He never gets nervous because of situations and circumstances. He is never prone to confusion. Also, God has His very best reasons for what He does and allows.

985. God really wants service out of great gratitude for love.

986. God wants us wealthy so we can destroy poverty once and for all.

987. War is also called "political famine."

988. Defilement of the land includes bloodshed, idolatry, and broken covenants. We must repent of this. Curses are alive upon land that is defiled. Pray: "Lord, please forgive the iniquities that have happened here, please Lord, in Jesus' name Amen." You may have to pray this prayer for a while, but keep praying.

989. A smile on your face sows kindness, gentleness, respect, and acceptance. It causes people to relax, lay down their defenses, and be comfortable. You can also smile with your eyes.

990. Don't try to fix everyone; just try to encourage them; they need people to believe in them.

991. Watch careless words and actions; they destroy relationships.

992. To inspire confidence, you must believe in what you are saying to others. This means you must speak with confidence.

993. A rare gift is always behind fear and opposition.

994. The greatest fear about people is that you will find out the truth about them.

995. Bitterness will cause speech defilement; it will darken your days, cause blind expectations, sop strength, destroy hope, cause self-deception, delusion, unhappiness, and make everyone around you that way.

996. The best ways to pull others toward you is to be an optimist, self-confident, excited person, interested in many things, and have a certain independence and an ability to go unconnected until a job is done, if it be so.

997. Jealousy is mostly fear turned around.

998. Don't let past failures make you an emotional wreck.

999. Never be afraid of failure, but do be afraid of succeeding in things that won't make a difference.

1000. Friendship requires long talks, cultivation, and walks over the years.

1001. A gentle tongue is a tree of life with healing power.

1002. The perfect will of God is to get His wisdom and apply it.

1003. God is morally excellent.

1004. Now that you know God loves you, you can love sacrificially, unselfishly, unconditionally, inexhaustibly, and unreservedly.

1005. How often shall a person forgive? Until it stops hurting. Forgiveness will rid hatred, malice, resentment, and the giving up of all claims of being compensated.

1006. Your response to offenses shows your level of maturity.

1007. There are those that may not be loving simply because something in the past has severely wounded their spirit. There is always more than what meets the eye.

1008. Wickedness always uses temptation, accusation, and intimidation to stop you.

1009. Temptation can also manifest in these five forms: depression, despair, resignation, failure, and inferiority. Be ready to prevail against them all.

1010. Prayerlessness is also a form of hiding.

1011. Don't miss your place in the lineage of Christ through impatience, giving up, and unbelief.

1012. Right relationships provide a protective covering over you. That is why evil intentions seek to divide and conquer.

1013. Manners make a person beautiful. They are essential for a child's self-confidence and success in life. Manners give you favor with people as well. The absence of manners and respect prevents people from wanting to be in your company.

1014. Evil uses the following tactics to keep you in error: noise, which causes you to not think clearly; staying in a hurry, which causes you to make wrong decisions; and associating with the crowds, which never means that the crowds are led by the right people.

1015. The Old Testament Law made us aware of sin but wasn't given the means to destroy it. But the New Testament gave us the means and ability through Christ to destroy sin in our life. Jesus provides the power.

1016. Abomination also includes attitudes and actions that are disgusting, offensive, and hateful to God, a disgrace, horrible, outrageous, and curse causing.

1017. A lazy person is a wasteful person, especially with his time.

1018. Patience comes from the Latin word that means to suffer, do it without complaint; it must happen so one can grow in patience and stay in control. A leader can calmly tolerate trouble while refusing to be propelled by it. Never tolerate abuse.

1019. We must learn to subject the material, human, and physical world to God's spiritual world.

1020. There is a divine special interest in the way the community treats its most vulnerable members, widows and resident aliens.

1021. We all should want to be perfect in knowledge, rich with perfect wisdom, and have levels of perfect understanding.

1022. When the world walks in complete disobedience, it brings a drought upon the land. The land suffers, the animals and fish suffer, the water dries up, and the wild beast and the birds suffer as well.

1023. One of the main keys of life is to properly discern and understand the Spirit world. The Bible is the only correct source of balance and true reference. Any other source brings great error, confession, traps, and extreme detriment to your life.

1024. Marriage will bring out what's wrong with you. Correct it. To thy own self, be true.

1025. When we find wisdom, we find the favor of God. The blessings of God are also called the "mansions of joy."

1026. Be one who wants to lead people and communities into the regions of honor and joy. God's Word is the only viable foundation upon which to build a moral system.

1027. A worldly man has many joys and carnal delights, which all are vain, false, and empty.

1028. Breathing lies continuously will prove to be like inhaling poison.

1029. Working more than sixty hours a week can cause a 60 percent jump in cardiovascular issues, relational problems, and a decrease in productivity.

1030. Why is it so important to study origins and where we came from? Well, if you think you came from a big bang with no purpose, then life will feel like you have no meaning. But, when you know God created everything with purpose and meaning, then you would also realize you are here for a reason and created for a purpose. Stress is a normal part of everyday life. When we allow it to *exceed its limits,* however, that's when we break or blow a fuse physically, emotionally, and mentally. Everyone is under a certain amount of daily stress.

1031. Your body talks to you through little unusual signs, saying, "I'm going into overload." Therefore, get somewhere, be peaceful and sit down for about fifteen minutes and you can be refreshed. (Don't ignore when your body begins to talk to you through physical and mental warnings. You may want to see your doctor immediately.)

1032. When you continue to practice wrong actions in life, you bring upon yourself unlimited and very harmful mental and physical stresses. Therefore many people anesthetize themselves with drugs, excessive drinking, uncontrollable sexual habits, and so on.

1033. Some of the very best ideas come from shy people.

1034. Listening to children helps raise their self-esteem.

1035. Anger is a normal human emotion; we must, however, learn how to control it.

1036. Don't put down other people just to place the spotlight on you.

1037. You can be a product of your response rather than your surroundings.

1038. When you interrupt conversations, it can show low self-esteem. Always compliment yourself on excellent efforts.

1039. Don't try to be just like someone else; develop your own interest and skills.

1040. Each success builds the confidence to strive for another. You will *feel* successful when you achieve each and every goal.

1041. Self-confidence provides power to go after the next endeavor.

1042. Studies prove that parents and teachers, not peer pressure, are children's strongest influence.

1043. We talk to ourselves, whether we know it or not; though people can speak with their mouths at the rate of 150 to 200 words per minute, we carry an inner dialogue at the rate of 1300 words per minute. This, in a dialogue, is called "self-talk." This is why we must encourage ourselves much more than be critical and hard on ourselves.

1044. The following messages are those that we believe, and they are lies that produce self-esteem. They also produce depression, anxiety, self-defeat, lack of confidence, distortions, and failures: 1) I need to be loved by everyone; 2) It's terrible when things are not precisely the way I want them; 3) It's better to avoid my problems than to face them; 4) I must be totally competent in every situation, and 5) I must completely be self-controlled at all times.

1045. Your brain or your subconscious hold all the beliefs, attitudes, and expectations recorded during a lifetime. Some are right, and some are not.

1046. Your personality is the expression of who you are as an individual. However, your personality is to be enhanced through the best character traits possible. This will take a lifetime.

1047. Determining how you think about yourself also explains your level of self-esteem. Rather it's high or low.

1048. Your God expects you to become a very wise individual. The following words are associated with being wise: intelligence, cleverness, learned, astute, sharp, informed, canny, knowing, preceptor, insightful, smart, rational, farsighted, logical, strategic, sound, and sane.

1049. On the flip side, stupidity is associated with words like foolish, dazed, unintelligent, unable to think clearly, idiot, slow, dopey, naive, crazy, lame brain, scatterbrained, dumb, gullible, Ludacris, ridiculous, futile, insane, senseless, batty, nutty, and out to lunch.

1050. Gambling feeds upon human weaknesses and contributes to the desire to get something for nothing. This attitude encourages faith in chance. This attitude also breeds fraud, dishonesty, and crime, and it severely damages character.

1051. Loving yourself will include saying the same things to yourself that you would say to your very best friend if they messed up.

1052. Forgive yourself. Forgive every failure and all that has given you pain in the past. Remember, again, you are not the result of your mistakes, failures, and wrong attitudes.

1053. We are to be a community of care.

1054. Obeying laws creates good discipline.

1055. We easily say a lot of things, but we must begin to mean them all with sincerity.

1056. It is time out from being sincerely wrong to becoming sincerely right. Just because your heart is in the right place does not replace wisdom and support for ignorance.

1057. Haughtiness is your greatest enemy, and humility is your greatest friend.

1058. Never call people names that are improper, such as stupid, crazy, foolish, etc.

1059. Never let human opinion become your weakness.

1060. Holiness is not a list of rules to freeze freedom and crush creativity or steal your fun. When God says don't or thou shalt not, He really means "don't hurt yourself." Holiness is joy-producing, and this joy is infinite and eternal.

1061. Many are searching and looking for something that fulfills them. My question to you is, are you trying to find your way back home?

1062. God is as close to you as your lips; He's also seated in heaven, secure, settled, not wrangling his hands, pacing back and forth; He is in full control and never worried. Everyone in the throne room of God knows this. He is not the man upstairs with a white beard; He is ineffable, divine, beyond words, indescribable, and heavenly.

1063. When you get jealous, make a list of the things that you are grateful for and the things that you have accomplished, successes, and possessions you have. This will help you.

1064. Stop looking at victory for other people as losses to you. Be glad for everyone because your day is coming. If you don't, you will stay in continual frustration, and you will choose to be completely unhappy. Share and genuinely celebrate others' successes.

1065. A meek and quiet spirit is one of great price.

1066. A significant amount of freedom and liberation comes through submitting to rules and regulations. The root of awesome character is in keeping God's commandments. Jesus was more concerned about the prize of pleasing God; we should do too.

1067. For couples, continue to love your mate even when they are not responding like they should. Honoring them also means listening to and respecting their opinions. When people are making positive changes, encourage them.

1068. Choose to love through tough times.

1069. What you say to people represents your mind and your heart.

1070. Being a gentleman, men, and being a lady, women, represents and starts with how you treat yourself. Refine yourself to the fullest potential.

1071. Self-confidence takes off when you know a lot about many things. Your passion lights up with pride, self-respect, and deep admiration. Your developed professional abilities and qualities will add to this as well.

1072. The more you pursue wisdom, the more your life will have more meaning.

1073. Satan and demonic spirits are the cause of isolation, confusion, sleeplessness, suicide, and the repeating of the past over and over again.

1074. Encourage your friends with the power of your presence and always tell them that they are important to you.

1075. We all will walk in complete unity when we accept the characteristic traits of God.

1076. We were all made to be relational and not to be on our own.

1077. The greatness of life will come from character, relationships, family, and friends, and it will impact the entire quality of your life.

1078. Research indicates that 85 percent of people are fired because of lack of relational skills, not technical.

1079. No matter what work you do, we should always have loving God and caring for others to be the center of it.

1080. The following are cues of success: How well did your kids turn out? Did I live a rich and fulfilling life? Did I positively change lies? Did I build deep and meaningful relationships? Did I really love my spouse? Did I make a difference?

1081. Be responsible for your attitudes, beliefs, and commitments.

1082. Using these wisdoms will guarantee a pattern of success and excellence.

1083. Fulfillment begins when life is meaningful. If you don't indulge in purpose, you will stay dissatisfied. The church can help you find God's purpose for your life.

1084. No matter how the public is changing, stay unified with righteousness.

1085. Fifty-five percent of houses have very few books in them.

1086. Every person in this world has a personal ministry from God, meaning something God wants them to serve.

1087. The church is the most powerful organization in the world because Jesus started it.

1088. Protestants are responsible for creating peaceful and wealthy societies. Scientists and historians agree that the preaching of protestant preachers is responsible for today's civilizations.

1089. It's said that people will depend more on your character than your IQ. Jack Erwood said that the world was built to depend on character.

1090. Be careful; this society will teach, breed, and trap you into being discontent. Innumerable commercials are designed to keep you dismayed, dissatisfied, unhappy, and a mess to live with.

1091. Thankfulness has proven to help you in practically every arena of health and life. It makes you optimistic, lowers blood pressure, produces happy hormones, decreases depression, enhances your love life, induces relaxation, and boosts your immune system.

1092. Even the most difficult times come with some benefit. Look how people come together to help one another.

1093. Consider for a moment how others have been blessed by you. Let their joys and appreciation bless your heart. Yes, to God be all the glory, but you had a lot to do with it. Receive this encouragement. You need and deserve it.

1094. God wants us to have the same faith and confidence in His Word as He does.

1095. Kings and priests, know for a surety that when you declare a decree, you make a law in heaven.

1096. The Hebrew word for "*holy*" is the same derivative for the word "*wedding.*"

1097. Transformation and positive change mainly do not happen at church; it's designed to happen more so when you use the principles at home and during the week.

1098. Relational maturity is found (only) when righteous principles are vividly evident.

1099. Be kind and forgiving with your family. You really will need them later in life.

1100. God actually experiences us when we worship Him. Worship is really a lifestyle.

CPSIA information can be obtained
at www.ICGtesting.com
Printed in the USA
LVHW040829301022
731860LV00006B/21